More Praise for *How to Change Minds*

"How do we discern whether we are unwittingly manipulating someone when our intention is simply to influence? Enter Rob Jolles. A
sought-after speaker with a background in sales and training, Rob is
an expert not only in the art of influence but also in human nature.
How to Change Minds coaches readers on the fine point of *ethical*
persuasion—*the art of influence without manipulation*. If you want
to change minds the right way, reading this book is the right thing
to do."
—**Ken Blanchard, coauthor of *The One Minute Manager* and *Trust
Works!***

"This book takes you on a wonderful journey to greater understanding
of how to persuade while transcending the boundaries of traditional
selling and into the heart and mind of anyone who needs to influence
behavior."
—**Brian Tracy, author of *Eat That Frog!***

"The wisest and most ethical sales trainers share a common goal with
psychotherapists—to facilitate their clients' change in ways that will
help them achieve the success they seek. Rob Jolles's approach will
help show you how!"
—**Cliff Ayers, PhD, clinical psychologist**

"Learning to influence behavior is a powerful skill that all members in
the law enforcement community should master. It's a tool used each
and every time we get that call for a barricade or hostage situation.
This book will assist all in the law enforcement community with their
day-to-day operations, and I would encourage all my colleagues to
read this book."
—**Bill Soper, Assistant Commander, Calvert County Sheriff's Office**

"Rob Jolles once again identifies nuanced elements of the selling process no one else sees and presents specific actions selling professionals can take to grow their business. We will be recommending this
book to our members."
—**Fred Diamond, cofounder, Institute for Excellence in Sales & Business
Development**

"As salespeople, we constantly find ourselves walking the fine line between 'creating urgency' and 'being pushy.' The former is of tremendous importance to any salesperson, while the latter can be disastrous. Rob Jolles examines the nuances of this fine line, offering a unique perspective for anyone to follow. This is truly the microscopic DNA that separates the rock stars from the also-rans in the world of sales."
—**Jim Wolf, Vice President for Sales, TeleVox Software**

"Persuasion without a moral compass is an altogether too common form of communication in today's hectic, technology-based world, where the sound bite and the political gotcha dominate over real dialogue. Experience, clarity of expression, and decades' worth of teaching relationships have given Rob the insight to write such a book, and I recommend it to anyone seeking answers on this important topic."
—**Robert "Frank" Muller Jr., CEO, Behringer Securities**

"The ideas and lessons taught in this book and what Rob has taught many of us for decades on how to influence change have proven to be endless in application. Whether you are consulting with clients, negotiating a deal, leading a team of people, or dealing with your children, it works!"
—**Glenn M. Cackovic, Managing Partner, GlobalMacro Capital Management, LLC**

"Rob creates entire new systems in the way we think—and if we allow it, it won't just change our client interactions; it has the power to change our marriage and our friendships for the better. My ability to listen, understand, and influence people for *good* has been revolutionized since being introduced to his concepts."
—**Nic Heywood, Wealth Management Advisor, TIAA-CREF**

HOW *to* CHANGE MINDS

HOW *to*
CHANGE
MINDS

The Art of Influence without Manipulation

ROB JOLLES

Reprinted with permission of Berrett-Koehler by Network TwentyOne International, 2014.

Berrett-Koehler Publishers, Inc.
235 Montgomery Street, Suite 650
San Francisco, CA 94104-2916
Tel: (415) 288-0260   Fax: (415) 362-2512   www.bkconnection.com

Berrett-Koehler and the BK logo are registered trademarks of Berrett-Koehler Publishers, Inc.

Printed in the United States of America

Library of Congress Cataloging-in-Publication Data

Jolles, Robert L., 1957-
  How to change minds : the the art of influence without manipulation / Rob Jolles. — First edition.
      pages cm
    Includes index.
    ISBN 978-1-60994-829-0 (pbk.)
    1. Selling—Psychological aspects. 2. Change (Psychology) 3. Decision making—Psychological aspects. 4. Influence (Psychology) I. Title.
  HF5438.8.P75J667 2013
    302'.13—dc23   2013009364

First Edition
18 17 16 15 14 13   10 9 8 7 6 5 4 3 2 1

This book is dedicated to the greatest salesman who ever lived. He was a man who could change a mind in a heartbeat, with the skill of a surgeon. What I learned, I learned from him, and what I write, I write for him. Xerox taught me how, but he taught me why. He was my father. Rest easy, Lion Lee Jolles; your voice and words will never be forgotten.

Contents

Preface   ix

1   Changing Minds—Changing Lives   1

2   Inside the Minds of Those You Are Changing   17

3   Establishing Trust   39

4   The Blueprint for Changing Minds   57

5   Committing to Change   85

6   Initiating Change   109

7   "I Object!"   127

8   How to Change *Your* Mind   149

Who Am I? A "Sto-em"   163

How to Change Minds Worksheet   169

Appendix: Influence without Manipulation   171

Acknowledgments   175

Index   177

About the Author   185

Preface

If I could show you a way, with 100 percent certainty, to maximize the odds of your ability to change another person's mind, would you jump at the opportunity to acquire these skills? Take a deep breath, and consider these words for a moment, because that's exactly what I can do. But there's a catch. Along with the skills you harness when you learn *how to change minds* comes a moral responsibility. In the words of Franklin Delano Roosevelt, Winston Churchill, and even Stan Lee (to mention a few):

With great power comes great responsibility.

Within the pages you are about to read, I am confident of two things. First, you will find a process that is repeatable, predictable, and allows you the best opportunity possible to change another person's mind. Second, you will find yourself in a front-row seat peering over a thin line that separates influence from manipulation. At times that line can become so thin that the only thing that distinguishes one from the other is sheer intent.

It will be my job not only to show you how to change minds, but to draw the boundaries between influence and manipulation. To succeed in such lofty goals, this book will have to deliver on four separate fronts: (1) It must be applicable to all, (2) it must be ethical, (3) it must be measurable, and (4) it must be something *you* believe in.

IT MUST BE APPLICABLE TO ALL

After nearly three decades of teaching people to sell, and transferring these skills to those who don't necessarily sell for a living, I've learned that the topic of persuasion can create some immediate anxiety. There are two questions that should be on your mind, to address right out of the gate.

The first is, Do you have to be a salesperson to use these skills? It would be trite to repeat the words you've probably heard over and over again: "Everybody sells." However, for many who simply want to apply selling skills to a child being parented, a cherished friend who needs to change his or her ways, or a manager who wants to change the ways of the team, this question can be haunting.

The processes we will explain are demonstrably and effectively used by professional salespeople. However, for decades I have conducted workshops and taught selling skills to NASA engineers, hostage negotiators, artists, parent groups, and many more. Learning how to change minds is not an exclusive skill available only to those who sell for a living. The act of influence has no boundaries.

The second question you should ask is, Do you have to possess certain natural skills to be effective at influencing others? This question can be rephrased many different ways, for example, "Are you born a salesperson?" or "Can anybody do this?" But any way you slice it, the question remains essentially the same: "Can I learn to do this?" If I had a nickel for every time I have been asked this question, well, let's just say, I'd have a heck of a lot of nickels!

I didn't know the answer myself until I was fortunate enough to meet one of the greatest salesman who ever lived. He wasn't a big-shot author (a fraternity I know all too well). No, he was a rather quiet, unassuming man named Ben Feldman.

It's Just a Question of Style

You probably haven't heard of him either, so let me introduce you. In 1979, my first year out of college, and my first year with the New York Life Insurance Company, Ben led the industry in sales. Actually, it is inadequate to say he led the industry. He dominated it, with a lifetime total of $1.6 billion in sales. Out of a pool of close to a quarter of a million salespeople, the sales numbers of the top nine agents were fairly close to one another. Ben Feldman's totals were triple those of his next closest competitor.

I had never met Ben, but I imagined him to be outgoing, tall, and aggressive, with a big, booming voice. I guess I saw him as a collection of every stereotype I had been led to believe comprised an effective salesperson. The day I had the rare pleasure of meeting this man, he changed my life.

Ben Feldman stood about five feet three inches, a somewhat large fellow, with hair a little like Larry from The Three Stooges, and he spoke with a heavy lisp—not quite what I had expected. Within seconds, however, I was drawn to Ben Feldman's unique style. He had none of the more conventional strengths that we associate with his kind of success, yet he remained true to his style, used *his* strengths, and was a giant in his field.

That was the moment I learned the most valuable lesson I would ever receive in my life regarding personal style. I could not *be* Ben Feldman, but I could focus on his technique and continue to ask myself, "How can I do that so it sounds like *me*?" What is my personal style? My strengths aren't Ben's strengths, but then again, Ben's aren't mine either.

Ben Feldman didn't just inspire a 21-year-old kid trying to find his way in the world of selling, he inspired the world with one simple message: If you remain true to the unique strengths you possess, and follow sound, proven techniques, there is no style of communication that cannot be successful.

Ben Feldman passed away in the summer of 1994, but not without leaving us a few final gifts. Ironically, he did not leave much in the way of process behaviors (a series of predictable actions), behind. His actual selling techniques were not well documented, and the rare speeches he gave provided more inspiration than instruction. However, in my mind, his greatest gift may have been one he never articulated. He taught us that if you commit to your own personal style, you can become as great as you want to be. "Can anybody do this?" *Absolutely!* The key is to separate style from technique.

IT MUST BE ETHICAL

There is a lot at stake as we continue to work our way through the act of changing another person's mind. My focus will be on the moral tug of war between our desire to influence change and our will to preserve our personal ethics.

Webster's defines the word "ethics" this way: "a system of moral values." There isn't a whole lot of gray area here. Either you adhere to a system of moral values, or you don't; it's as simple as that. Or is it? When we are emotionally invested in creating change, even the most well-intentioned individuals can inadvertently struggle with the choices at hand.

Rather than ignore this potential conflict, I want to examine how well-intentioned people can find themselves challenged to do the right thing. By doing so, I believe we can step out of the shadows of feeling that changing someone's mind by applying the skills of influence is somehow a bad thing. It isn't. In fact, it can provide one of the greatest acts act of kindness one human being can extend to another. On the other hand, changing someone's mind by applying the skills of manipulation can be a despicable act of selfishness, and that's why we must start here.

You see, most of us don't wake up one day, stretch, grab a cup of coffee, and say to ourselves, "You know, I feel like being unethical today." It's a little more complicated than that. In fact, it begins with another word we'll now introduce. The word is "justification," which *Webster's* defines this way: "a reason, fact, circumstance, or explanation that justifies or defends."

As a professional speaker and author who studies and writes about human behavior, I can tell you that people do not set out to be unethical. However, when you have a lucrative, possibly career-changing sales contest victory within an inch of your grasp, the line between influence and manipulation stands out in boldface. When you have a companion whose change of behavior would result more in our personal gain than in his or hers, that line appears again. Mix in the word "justification," and you have a recipe for unethical behavior.

The line is easy for you to distinguish, you say? Well, we all have our ethical thresholds. For instance, if you were in a library and found a beautiful Montblanc pen that had been left behind at the table, would you take it to the Lost and Found? Maybe. Now let's sprinkle in a little bit of "justification." What if you had been given a beautiful Montblanc pen as a token of thanks for your participation in a meaningful event, and you had left it behind a month ago, and it had not been returned to you? As you sit in the library and roll this new pen between your fingers, will you still run to the Lost and Found to return it? After all, someone took your beautiful Montblanc pen; shouldn't you be able to keep this pen, to replace it? It seems only fair. That's what I mean by justification.

One of my unique clients was a group of more than 650 polygraph examiners. I learned from these fine folks that regardless of the crime, the confessions always contained an almost bizarre sense of justification. "I know I embezzled the money, but I had two tuitions to pay, the owner has more money than he knows what to do with, and he left the safe open!" I know it's easy for you and me to see this for what it is, which is stealing, but the person who was confessing *justified* this lack of ethics and saw it as a way to survive.

It is clearly the norm, not the exception, to justify any questionable act we may engage in, and this dilemma is by no means new. Case after case throughout history highlight this issue. John Wilkes Booth, who assassinated our beloved President Abraham Lincoln, did not in any way perceive his actions to be unjust. History tells us that Booth felt justified in his horrific act, believing that his actions would not only turn the tide of the Civil War, but would eventually make him a celebrated hero to all humankind.

We all need to be on guard when our inner voice of ethical guidance is countered by another voice that tries to rationalize a set of behaviors that, deep down, we know is not right. So our second hurdle will be to provide a line between when the skills of influence are appropriate, and when we cross that line into manipulation. This is why there will be reminders emphasizing just where lines between influence and manipulation exist, with the intention of protecting and guiding against inadvertently straying over the line.

IT MUST BE MEASURABLE

As you read this book, you'll find out soon enough that I enjoy telling stories, and at times I hope you find this book entertaining. Other times I think you might find what I write can be inspiring, and still other times you might even find it motivational. But if that's all, I've wasted your time. There's simply too much at stake here.

You see the problem at hand: I want you to demand more from me. Entertaining, inspiring, and motivating you are easy. Teaching you exactly *how to change minds* using the skills of influence *without* manipulation is the tough part. But that's exactly what you'll find within this book, and you'll find these tactics defined in an exact process.

When you have a process, you have a way of measuring what you are doing. When you can measure it, you can fix it.

Finding the Right Measurement

Selling for the New York Life Insurance Company was my first job out of school, and I think back fondly on those early days. I was young and motivated to succeed. The measurements that were laid out for me were simple ones. "Two sales a week, ten sales a month, and don't let us catch you hanging around the office waiting for the phone to ring!" I guess you could say that's one form of measurement.

Interestingly enough, by that form of measurement, I was a darned good insurance salesman. Some months my numbers were really good, and management would tell me, "Whatever you're doing, just keep doing it." Some months my numbers were not very good, and management's remarks weren't quite as generous. I had a nagging feeling there was something I was missing, but I also almost always hit those numbers by the measurement that was established for me, and I was therefore defined as a good salesman.

I had a good career with New York Life, and I will always be grateful to that company for giving me a chance to sell. However, it was frustrating to chase those numbers without really understanding what I was doing right or wrong, from a process standpoint, and eventually I left the company and joined Xerox.

New York Life taught me to *love* to sell, and then Xerox taught me *how* to sell. At Xerox, it seemed like you didn't tie your shoes without some kind of measurement, but therein lay the genius of Xerox.

Xerox was obsessed with the mechanics behind what we were doing at all times. Initially, they had no interest in how many sales I was making, but rather in the process I was following to make those sales. As a matter of fact, during the initial sales training with Xerox, which was considered some of the finest in the world, we never mentioned a copier. For training purposes, we sold answering machines and airplanes. The theory was, to perfect the process, the product itself was irrelevant.

With a repeatable, predictable, and, above all, measurable process in place, I no longer had the nagging feeling that I was missing something. When I sold well, I could tell you why, and when I didn't, I could tell you why. I have never forgotten the lessons Xerox taught me, and today I base a lot of what I teach on the principles they instilled in me.

※ ※ ※

The ultimate test of what you will be learning will not be whether you can understand what is being taught. The ultimate test will be whether you can implement what you have learned, and— with a repeatable, predictable, process that you can measure—that's exactly what you will be equipped to do.

IT MUST BE SOMETHING *YOU* BELIEVE IN

When you stop and think about it, having the ability to change another person's mind is pretty heady stuff. That's why the moment we end this preface, we will start a conversation designed to help you understand exactly why it takes courage to use these skills. I suppose it would be easy to step away from the controversy of influence, and let people simply change their minds and behaviors without our help. But doing so leaves people vulnerable to one of the most pervasive fears anyone can face: the fear of change.

Years ago, *The Book of Lists** produced a rather famous collection of fears that surprised many of us when the top five turned out to be:

1. Speaking before a group
2. Heights
3. Insects and bugs
4. Financial problems
5. Deep water

Newer lists have come out since, with few changes, other than the fear of flying, making their way into the top

*David Wallechinsky et al.: *The Book of Lists* (New York: Wm. Morrow & Co., Inc.).

five. However, I maintain there is another fear that doesn't appear on any list and yet is a stumbling block for us all. What's more, it is a far more personally destructive fear. I'm referring to the *fear of change*.

Think back on your life and how often you have been faced with a challenging decision. You no doubt weighed your options, and both logic and instinct presented you with a solution. Then, you did what so many of us are guilty of doing: nothing. The fear of change not only overpowered your reasoning, it left you with a frustrating reminder when you finally did get around to making a decision. Your souvenir was the phrase that came out like a mantra: "I wish I had done it sooner."

The fear of the unknown often outweighs the pain of the present.

The solution comes from your ability to stay away from solving others' problems for them, and focusing instead on leading them to solve their own problems. People rarely look down the road at the impact of their problems; if they did, we would not have to engage in these challenging conversations. We would not have to seek someone out, set up a meeting, or plan a phone call, because those you would be aiming to influence would be calling you. There is a solution. If you want to defuse fear of change, it all hinges on your ability to embrace the skills of influence.

You don't need to apologize or excuse yourself for leading someone on a path of change. As you will read in the pages that follow, under the proper circumstances, guiding people past their fear of change can be one of the most meaningful acts of kindness you could ever offer another individual. Still, some people just don't get it.

Some years ago, minutes before a keynote speech I was to deliver, I had an interesting, perhaps even inspirational, moment. As a creature of habit, before a presentation I typically like to pace around quietly and keep to myself. While outside getting into my speaker zone (if you will), I ran into an interesting individual.

I was alone in the hallway except for a woman who was also pacing around a bit, and she didn't look very happy. I was curious, so I struck up a conversation. I asked her how she was doing, and that's all it took to get her going.

"How am I doing, you ask? I'm miserable. In about five minutes I've got to go into that room, sit for an hour, and listen to some jerk talk to me about selling! Can you believe it?"

Before I could even speak, she just kept going. "I wouldn't be here if my manager wasn't making me attend this fiasco. I've never liked salespeople, and now I've got to sit and listen to someone who actually teaches salespeople. What a colossal waste of time!" At that point an announcement interrupted her diatribe.

No, I did not single this woman out and confront her in front of 500 people in that hotel ballroom. Please, I'm a professional. However, I always speak with a wireless microphone so I can move around the room, and for some reason I not only wandered to exactly where this woman was sitting, but I delivered about 55 minutes of my 60-minute keynote address about a foot and a half from her ear.

Late that night, on a red-eye back to the East Coast, I found myself going back to that moment in the hallway. It bothered me to know that not only did this woman not really understand how vital to society those who know *how to change minds* are, but that she was by no means alone in her misconception.

The tray table came down, the laptop opened up, and the words began to fly as I began to craft my rebuttal. To this day I'm not exactly sure what I created. It's not exactly a story, and not exactly a poem. That's why I've always called it my "sto-em," and you can find it on page 165, where it can serve as a succinct summary of all the guideposts this book is about to describe, for influencing without manipulation.

You've done your job. You took a leap of faith, and you bought this book. Now it's time for me to do my job. Keep going, and you won't just be learning a new set of skills. You will be learning exactly how to assist others who struggle through change. It's time to learn *how to change minds*.

1

Changing Minds—
Changing Lives

*At its core, when you are applying influence and changing
another person's mind, you are taking an idea, planting that
idea in his brain, and making him feel as if he thought of it.*

Does the quote above disturb you? I'd be surprised if
it didn't. Let's not waste any time and get right to the
heart of the matter. Does that quote define influence or
manipulation? Indiana poet James Whitcomb Riley coined
the phrase, "When I see a bird that walks like a duck and
swims like a duck and quacks like a duck, I call that bird a
duck." I will show you a repeatable, predictable approach
to changing another person's mind. It's not always pretty,
it's not always safe, and I'm well aware that the use of the
word "influence" bothers people. The use of the word
"manipulation" sickens people. Worst of all, the line between
these two words can be razor thin. In fact, at times the
difference may very well come down to intent, and nothing
more. But before you shoot the messenger, please consider
the following story.

UNAVOIDABLE CONSEQUENCES

It's Tuesday morning, and Dan is running a little late for his annual physical. He's been seeing his doctor on a yearly basis for over a decade. As he puts the key in the ignition, he smiles and thinks, "I know how this is going to go."

Sitting in the examining room waiting for his doctor gives Dan a little time to reflect on the year since his last visit. He promised to take off some weight. Instead he has put on a few pounds. He promised to exercise more. He has been exercising less. Business is tough, and who has time to exercise? Besides, he's exhausted by the time he gets home from work.

When Dan's doctor finally does appear, the appointment, and the lecture that go with it, don't disappoint. "Dan, you need to make certain lifestyle changes!" Dan nods and promises he will, but deep down both men know that no changes will take place. They are both wrong.

Two months later it starts with a shortness of breath, and some pressure in Dan's chest, which goes away as fast as it started. Then the shortness of breath and pressure recur, escalating rapidly to discomfort in one of his arms, and nausea. His wife rushes him to the hospital where Dan's life is saved.

Of course, the double bypass he must endure is more brutal than he ever could have imagined. The missed work, the rehab, and the financial issues with an operation like this are also part of Dan's story. Today, my friend Dan is doing well. Not surprisingly, he's finally taken the weight off, and he has developed a steady and disciplined exercise routine.

This kind of frank and harsh scenario plays itself out over and over again, every day of the week, every week of the year, and every year of a lifetime. Sometimes it's a different vice, or no vice at all. It can be as simple as a poor study habit, or as complicated as an emotional scar stemming from a dysfunctional childhood. The players change, and certain elements of the plotline change, but the results are the same. And there's often a sense that there's nothing we can do about it. But I believe we *can* do something about it, and I want to show you exactly how.

In the early nineties when I was still with Xerox, my job was to work with outside clients who wanted to learn how to persuade the "Xerox way." I saw all kinds of clients you would not necessarily connect to selling, who had no difficulty connecting to the message of changing minds. However, a favorite client was one of the nation's largest churches. The story was the same, but substitute someone who has lost herself morally with someone who lost himself to alcohol. I was hearing the same story with a different client:

"We want to help people find their way. Unfortunately, those who really need us don't want our help." (You probably know the rest of the story.) "It seems that those who do want our help and are seeking us out always seem to be coming as a result of a recent tragedy in their lives."

What a coincidence. Or is it? The church in question became one of my best clients. Why? Because in less than five minutes I was able to convince the ministry that to save people, they had to stop preaching, and instead learn how to influence behavior and give the plotlines they were describing a good, old-fashioned *push*. When I formally taught them how to persuade, they succeeded, and are now one of the largest churches in the country.

Now notice, I didn't say "pitch," I said "push." So many people get squeamish when they hear the word "push." It sounds like you are shoving people toward a solution they cannot seem to find on their own. Guilty as charged; that's exactly what I'm proposing. Boiled down, we are often faced with only two choices: Either *pitch* a solution to someone, or *push* someone toward it. The focus of this book is a defense of the latter, because when it comes to changing minds, I'm no fan of the pitch.

IT'S NOT A "PITCH," IT'S A "PUSH"

I received an email from a good friend who asked me what I thought of the word "pitch." She was relating it to a salesperson she worked with who had an uncanny way of using the word to describe his daily sales activities, reveling in it every time. Never shy, I presented my opinion in three words: "I hate it." I can hear my mother now: "Hate is such a strong word." So, out of respect for my mother, let me put it this way: "I'm offended by it."

Let's do a little test. What is the first thing that comes to your mind when you hear the word "pitch"? Something tells me your first thought is not "ask questions" or "listen." Maybe I'm too emotional here, so let's consult *Webster's*, which defines "pitch" as a high-pressure sales talk.

Imagine setting up a meeting with a client, or phoning a friend to say, "For the record, I intend to have a high-pressure sales talk with you." Sounds like a surefire approach to getting the click of a hang-up in your ear. I suppose you could just surprise your friend with your pitch, but I think you get the point here. If this is something we have no intention of doing, and it's offensive to anyone you speak with, why is this word still even in use?

I suppose the word "pitch" has its place on QVC or on a good infomercial. The late Billy Mays was one of the best pitchmen who ever lived. I never got the sense that sitting with Billy would provide much back-and-forth banter, nor did I see him as a champion consultant, but, man, that guy could pitch! In fact, he was the perfect pitchman. He could outtalk, outshout, and outlast anyone who stepped up to his booth. I would not recommend stepping in front of another human being you want to persuade and shouting, "HI, ROB JOLLES HERE, AND DO I HAVE A SOLUTION FOR YOU!"

The irony here is that true influence in its purest form could not be further from the concept of a pitch. In fact, it's the complete opposite. Instead of talking, it involves listening. Instead of hammering on a one-idea-fits-all concept, it involves shaping the solution to fit another person's specific needs. Instead of obsessing on a solution, it involves studying another person's potential problems.

Want to know why salespeople get a bad name? It's because clients are afraid they are going to have to talk on the phone, or sit face-to-face with some knucklehead who wants to *pitch* something to them.

Long before my time, door-to-door salespeople (think Fuller Brush, vacuum cleaners, the Bible) roamed the earth, managed to get a foot in the door, and occasionally wowed someone with a well-rehearsed pitch. But the yellow leisure suits that accompanied that age of selling have gone out of style, and we've moved on. So let me finish this small tirade with a pitch of my own.

> Step right up, make a commitment, and join the millions who have said, no to the word "pitch"! Eliminate that word from your vocabulary and you'll not only spare yourself the embarrassment of informing others that you have little to no interest in their needs, you'll demonstrate a true understanding of what your real role is in the first place. (Do it today, and I'll even throw in a spiral slicer . . . but you must act now!)

As a parent, spouse, manager, or friend, our part of the plotline is always the same. We *want* to influence behavior, and we *want* to help, but we just don't know how. It's a fascinating paradox because we know what the solution is! It's so clear to us! We often rehearse what we need to say. Once we say it, we are hurt, if not shocked, that our well-rehearsed words seem to have no effect on the person we are trying to help. The reason for this is that most of us don't know how to give those we are trying to help the *push* they so desperately need. We don't know how to change minds.

Is it because we don't believe we have the right to do so, ethically? There is a moral line between influence and manipulation, but before we discuss it, let me repeat, you must believe that "influence" is not a bad word. It all begins with believing.

There can be no substitutes, no do-overs, no thinking about it. You must *believe in your solution.*

Why do I tell you this? Because, before we can start our journey to influence, we must create a foundation from which to begin. That foundation is based on belief. Ask yourself this simple question: "Do I believe, without a shadow of a doubt, in what I am prepared to influence another person to do?"

Sound corny? I hope not, because it's one of the most important questions you can ever ask yourself. I'm about to take you on a journey that will unlock doors that have been previously closed to you. My commitment to you is not only to teach you to influence others, but to give you tools that will be repeatable and predictable. But there's a catch. You must *believe* in what you are influencing others to do.

A Crisis in Believing

I'll warn you in advance, this is personal. When it comes to examining the art of influencing, we have a crisis, and it's a crisis in believing. So many struggle with the thought of influencing another person's actions. We should never, ever avoid the word "influence" again; we should respect it, embrace it, and believe in it.

The thought of using a set of skills to persuade others to do something based on your thoughts and not on theirs seems to make people nervous. I think we need to step up, get past our fears, and believe, because there are scenarios that exist that desperately require the skills of influence.

Left to our own devices, we are a species who instinctively fear change. We are a species who instinctively avoid the thought of long-term ramifications of a particular problem. We are a species who would rather dabble in the dysfunctional known, than risk venturing into the unknown.

We need to believe. We need to believe that the act of influence is not a skill that should be ridiculed or questioned. It should be inspected, respected, and, dare I say it, admired. But it starts with believing.

Believing there is a desperate need for people who can save us from our inability to question ourselves. Yes, there are scenarios begging for these skills.

There is a murky line between the art of influence and the act of manipulation. When you see the scenarios that demand influence, and the line that exists between that and manipulation, you will no longer fear the act of influence. You will believe.

ONE MORE SALES STORY

I knew a young man years ago who attended the University of Maryland. He was one heck of a salesman, and he wanted nothing more than to follow in the footsteps of his father, also a great salesman. As a kid, he had sold more light bulbs for his Cub Scouts' fund raiser than anyone else.

When he was old enough, he joined the Boy Scouts. His troop sold first-aid kits for the glove boxes of automobiles. His troop sold fertilizer. His troop even sold doughnuts door to door. No matter what the item was, this kid sold more than anyone else, and there were over 130 scouts in that kid's troop!

In high school he sold toothbrushes, and in college he sold shoes. He always took home the number one prize in sales.

He loved selling so much that when he graduated from the University of Maryland, he went on to work for the top insurance company in the country. Two weeks after turning 22 years old, he started selling insurance. He studied his sales scripts until he knew them cold, and most important of all, he believed in the product (after all, at some point life everyone needs life insurance).

He wanted to sell to older individuals because they were clients with defined needs. Unfortunately, though, his age held him back. He did not have a lot in common with older clients, so, at the suggestion of his managers, he worked diligently at selling to his peer group—other 22-year-olds. He struggled with the concept of selling life insurance to his peer group because there just wasn't a need for his product.

- Would the product protect his clients' families? Sure, but almost all of his friends were single.

- Would the product protect his clients' homes? Sure, but almost all of his friends were too young to own a home.

- Would the rates go up? Sure, but not for another fifteen years.

His manager came up with a great idea. With a clever rider (optional add-on) to the policy, his clients could keep purchasing insurance over a set period of time without evidence of insurability. In other words, he learned how to insure his clients' insurability.

Did he truly believe this solution was in the best interest of his clients? For some that had a history of family illness, yes; however, for most of his prospective clients, no. Did he sell it? Yes, and a lot of it. Did it bother him to sell it? Not at first.

But then it did bother him. He did not believe in his product, and this ate away at him. His sales numbers were strong, but after a couple of years it ate away at him so much that it cost him his career. I should know, because I was that kid.

I thought I was influencing behaviors, but in reality, I was engaged in *manipulating* behaviors. What's the difference between *influence* and *manipulation?* We'll look at this question from many angles, but for now, let's start here.

Those who manipulate engage in persuasion regardless of their personal feelings about a solution.

Those who influence *engage in persuasion only if their personal feelings support their solution.*

In short, I believe manipulation is unethical influence. If you wouldn't buy an insurance policy, don't influence someone else to. If you think the person you are speaking to has needs that an insurance policy addresses, influence her to take action.

If you wouldn't join a gym, don't influence someone else to. On the other hand, if you think the person you are speaking to has issues that would be properly addressed by joining a gym, influence him to take action.

If you don't believe in what you are influencing others to do, it might not catch up with you today, or tomorrow, but one day you'll look in the mirror as I did, and you will struggle with what you see.

I desperately need you to believe. I need you to believe that your children, your spouse, your boss, your co-workers, your clients, your banker, your accountant, your lawyer, your patient, your peers, and your friends will be better off by being influenced by your words. If you believe that, and I mean *really* believe that, down to your very core, I'll be happy to show you exactly how. If not, you will be building a wall with no foundation, and eventually it will crumble.

Dave's Parents

There are so many beautiful chapters in our lives. We are born, our parents nurture us, and we grow. If we are truly blessed, we get to experience life with our parents as they grow old. But with that blessing comes the challenge that old age brings to life. How many of us have heard scenarios like this?

> My parents are now in their mid-80s. Dad has early signs of Alzheimer's, and Mom is becoming too frail to take care of him properly. I've tried to get them to sell their house and move into a more senior living environment, but despite their challenges they'll have none of it. As a matter of fact, they seem to think that I am not being a loyal son by even asking them to talk about it.

Before we get anywhere near a process, let's get a few final things straight. People may not ask others to change their minds, but they often *need* to have their minds changed. In Dave's story, a situation with a sadly predictable ending unfolds. The license will be revoked *after* the accident occurs. The house that his parents are clinging to, which represents their freedom, will be sold *after* an avoidable accident, and the sanctuary they created turns cruelly against them.

We seem to discount rather than respect those who possess the skills necessary to move others to change. As a person who has devoted more than half his life teaching others how to do this, you'll pardon me if I'm a bit offended by those who discount these skills. Someone who possesses these skills may become your most valuable asset someday; he may even save your life.

How do you define a good doctor? As a professional who has a good knowledge of the medical specialty she represents? On the surface I would tend to agree with you, but let's dig a little deeper than the mere medical certification.

What about this doctor's bedside manner? That's important because as patients we need to feel comfortable with someone with whom we are sharing personal, intimate information. Even more than that, I want a doctor who knows how to change minds!

I thought my personal doctor, John Valenti, summed it all up beautifully one day when I saw him for my annual physical. I was asking him about staying healthy, and he said, quite succinctly, "Listen, if you exercise, eat right, and try to reduce the amount of stress in your life, you are doing all the right things. After that, it's just a question of avoiding bad luck."

Truer words have rarely been spoken. Now you know the secret to a good life. All you need to do is act on the information Dr. Valenti has now given both of us.

We all would like to live a healthy lifestyle. Chances are, we'll feel better and live longer if we do. Sounds like a pretty good plan to me. So why do so many of us struggle with the things we know we need to do to enjoy this healthy lifestyle?

Exercise? We'll get around to it, but many of us have a lot on our plate, and we don't have the time to devote to regular exercise. Besides, a hard workout is not the most enjoyable moment of the day. Yes, it feels great when we finish, but so does our head after we stop banging it against a wall!

Diet? Most of us know what is good for us to eat and what isn't good for us to eat. Foods that are actually good for us typically don't taste as good as the ones that are not as good for us. Besides, it's more expensive to eat healthy foods.

Reduce stress? Maybe that's the grayest of the three criteria here, but by the time we are adults we know what stresses us and what reduces our stress. It's difficult finding a new job, and it's scary starting a new relationship.

The funny thing is that eventually we make some of these changes on our own. Consider these examples.

Exercise? When we get embarrassed at the company picnic because we can't make it once around the field, or keep up with our kids in a pickup game, or lose a game of tennis to an inferior athlete, we just might get angry enough to start working out.

Diet? When we can no longer fit into a favorite pair of pants, or our blood pressure rises to an unsafe level, we'll begin to watch what we eat.

Reduce stress? If we are lucky, and we make it through a medical scare, we'll consider making tough changes in our lifestyle.

But what about the doctor, the one with the good bedside manner? Wouldn't it be nice if she could truly convince us to change our lifestyle? The ones who can convince us to make changes know how to influence our behavior. The ones that cannot convince us to make changes know *what* to tell us we need to do—they have the medical training and the information—but not *how*; they have no influence on our behavior, and get in and out of an examination room in a hurry.

A doctor is only one example of the kind of person I'm talking about. It could also be the lawyer who gets us to see that we would be better off paying to build a better contract as we go into a deal than shirking on this step and end up instead fighting the lawsuit that results from the deal.

It could be the parent who gets his kids to see that putting the Nintendo down and reading a book would have stronger long-term benefits in life than waiting for the U.S.

Army to call looking for someone who can work a joystick under pressure.

It could be the accountant who gets us to see that it would be better to have a professional guiding your business through the whitewater of corporate tax requirements than a tax professional guiding your business through the long and costly ramifications of an audit.

It could be a business, a parent, a manager, a teacher, a friend, a coach, or anyone who needs to change another person's mind. There is no profession or person that cannot benefit from the process about to be revealed.

This process is irrelevant without a foundation. That foundation is the understanding that it's human nature to fear change, and that no change can take place in the absence of believing, *truly* believing, in the necessity of influence.

When you believe in a thing, believe in it all the way, implicitly and unquestionable.

—Walt Disney

So, do *you* believe? Do you believe that there are scenarios in life that require the skills of influence? Equally important, do you believe the solution you are drawing someone toward is truly in the best interest of the person whose mind you are changing? Assuming the answer is yes, we now have a foundation for *influence*, while avoiding *manipulation*. So now we can dive right into the steps necessary to create this change of mind. Right? No, first we must understand the process those you want to influence must go through to get to these steps. And that is where we begin.

2

Inside the Minds of Those You Are Changing

Those who manipulate *obsess on persuasive tactics they can follow.*

Those who influence *obsess on understanding the decision process followed by those they are persuading.*

F or over twenty-five years I have polled audiences regarding the unique decisions they make, and through various economic crises, a couple of wars, and a handful of other historic moments, I've learned one important thing: People go through repeatable, predictable steps when they make changes, regardless of the specifics of the decision in question. Understanding how people make decisions is critical when learning how to change minds and influence another's behavior. As with many great ideas, discovering this process was almost an accident.

THE DECISION CYCLE

I have learned many different sales tactics over the years. When I worked at New York Life, I learned the Live, Die,

Quit story, the Hundred Man story, and a few other impressive scripts. When I worked at Xerox, I learned SPIN: Selling, Strategic Selling, and a few other impressive processes. We were tasked with training the salespeople at the Xerox authorized dealerships who were selling our products. It would have been easy simply to teach them the same process the Xerox sales force was using. One small problem: The selling process we used was licensed to be taught only to Xerox personnel. Dealerships may have been authorized to sell Xerox products, but they were not Xerox personnel.

Unfortunately, Xerox did not own a sales process of its own at that time. They had owned a program of their own (Professional Selling Skills), but sold it off for a tidy profit. So, in 1986, with no existing sales process of our own, we set about to create a program that would truly belong to us. We wanted our program to be as progressive as possible, and we wanted to include every persuasive tactic we could imagine. When the smoke cleared, we had a repeatable and predictable process we could use to teach selling. But this exercise revealed a new question: What about the *customer*? Is there a repeatable, predictable process that customers go through when making a decision for change?

Once we began looking at the ways customers make decisions, we began to see definable stages and decision points. In addition to being fascinating, it forever changed the way I viewed the art of influence. Initially, it was referred to as a *buying cycle*. But the more companies I worked with, the more I knew we had to find a new name for a process that was more universal. With clients such as police departments, NASA engineers, teachers, lawyers, doctors, and others, I was working with people who did not think of themselves as *selling* anything. They did realize, however, that they were working with people who were struggling to make certain decisions. They were working with individuals who were demonstrating a true *decision cycle*.

The longer I have studied this side of the equation, the clearer the benefits have become. To this day, one of my favorite questions for an audience is this: Do you believe that people go through repeatable, predictable processes when they are making a decision? Interestingly enough, the audience's reaction is usually mixed. I follow up with this question: "Suspend your disbelief for a moment, and suppose I can prove to you this process does exist. If you're trying to help people make a change they are struggling with, wouldn't it be useful to understand the decision process they are going through, and where they are within that process?" I usually see some heads nodding at this point. This knowledge is more than an effective guide to working with others; it helps you find the appropriate tactics to assist others who are struggling with decisions.

The rest is history. The proof comes from the more than 50,000 people I have personally polled over the past twenty-five years regarding the decisions they have made. Knowing this not only helps you to see things from another person's perspective, it provides a window inside the minds you are changing.

I can't emphasize enough how important focusing from another person's perspective can be when changing minds. You don't believe a process like this exists? Let's see if we can prove it by relating it to your own life.

Consider the six stages I will now outline, and see if they resemble the process you followed as you made a recent important decision in your own life. While you track your example, I'll track an example of my own.

THE SATISFIED STAGE

Satisfied

Even in a repeatable cycle, there has to be a beginning, and the *satisfied stage* represents just that. In this stage of the cycle, individuals are convinced they have no needs, and no problems. In their minds, everything is perfect.

I'm all for more people in this world being happy and feeling everything's perfect; I just don't believe most people are telling the truth. Before you get upset about that, consider this question: What percentage of people are truly in the satisfied stage regarding events within their lives? 50 percent? 40 percent? 30 percent?

Allow me to separate facts from feelings. The real answer is somewhere between 4½ and 5 percent. Surprised?

Those are numbers I can support with decades of research. What I can't support is my feeling that this number is actually closer to 2 percent. I believe that fully half of those who say they are 100 percent happy with a given scenario are not lying; they are simply unaware.

How many times have we heard on the news that a particular product we thought was good for us was not good for us after all? Just because we are unaware of a problem doesn't mean the problem doesn't exist.

Our First House

Can you remember the first house you bought? I can sure remember mine. I was newly married, and my wife and I decided it was time to move from our condominium. It was a seller's market, and real estate was moving fast. It wasn't unusual to see a house go on the market, and within twenty-four hours have three or four contracts written at or above the asking price. We had lost one house we liked a lot because we were slow to put down a contract, so when we got word of a house that was going on the market in the morning, we came rushing in the night before. We wanted to be ready to move fast, and we did.

We saw a beautiful Cape Cod home in Bethesda, Maryland, which we fell in love with. The location was almost perfect. A few blocks inside the Capitol Beltway made it close to everything. We especially loved the quiet little cul-de-sac it was located on . . . on that particular day. It was our house, on a quiet little cul-de-sac, and we loved it!

✳ ✳ ✳

There may very well be issues to deal with in the future, but the satisfied stage represents a kind of honeymoon that decision makers reside in for a short period of time. Honeymoons don't last forever, and before too long we become aware that the decision we have made may not be perfect. That's when we make our first move within the cycle.

THE ACKNOWLEDGE STAGE

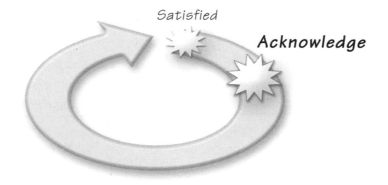

Satisfied

Acknowledge

And then the potential for change emerges. The *acknowledge stage* represents the most significant step relating to the way people make decisions, and it is the most critical element of the decision cycle. It is also the most misunderstood component.

Small Trouble in Paradise

As we rushed to put a contract down on this house, we didn't realize that we had viewed it at the height of rush hour. The

Capitol Beltway was at a standstill. What we quickly realized once our contract was accepted was that this house wasn't just *near* the Beltway, it sounded like it was *in* the Beltway! But this was our house, on a *sometimes* quiet little cul-de-sac, and we loved it.

* * *

The acknowledge stage represents a basic dichotomy in our mind. In this stage, we will readily admit that yes, we do have particular problems that *could* require change. Unfortunately, we will just as readily state no, we do not want to do anything about these problems at this time.

Many people with whom I work tell me that this is the place in the decision cycle where most of the people they are looking to influence seem to reside. According to my numbers, they happen to be absolutely right. Seventy-nine percent of the people I survey state that this is exactly where they are in the decision cycle "It hurts," they say, "but it doesn't hurt very much." There is no sense of urgency and, therefore, no serious interest in change.

I sometimes refer to this stage as the whining stage. Many of us whine incessantly but don't do anything to alter what we are whining about. Adding insult to injury, the vast majority of the population is not only locked into the acknowledge stage, but they are locked into it for a long time.

Bigger Trouble in Paradise

As the years went by, we were thrilled by the birth of our first child, and then our second. We were also thrilled by the techniques used to neutralize the noise from the Beltway. To combat the constant noise we kept our storm windows closed year-round, installed on our deck one of the first outside speakers Bose ever made, and even purchased a device I called our "sound-a-lizer." This was a particularly loud air cleaner we would turn on each night in our bedroom. We liked it so much, we even bought a second one because this was our house on a not-so-quiet little cul-de-sac, and we put up with the problems.

* * *

People don't fix small problems; they fix big ones.

Two things keep people paralyzed in the acknowledge stage. The first is the perceived size of the problem. Regardless of the problem, if people do not perceive the problem as a big one, they will feel no urgency to do anything about it. People procrastinate and put off acting on the difficulties they face. That's human nature, and that's what keeps us all pinned down in the acknowledge stage for long periods of time. As the problem grows in size, we begin to gravitate closer to a critical *decision point*. When the problem becomes too enormous, we cross over a kind of metaphorical line in the sand. This line represents a decision to make a change.

The second reason people remain in the acknowledge stage for so long is an issue that will come up a few more times in this book; the *fear of change*. Ultimately, this fear is often the one stumbling block that challenges even persuasive people. It may not seem fair, and it may not seem right, but this fear hides inside us all.

The fear of change often outweighs the pain of the present.

Seventy-nine percent of the people I surveyed represents a lot of opportunities, from a change perspective, and I can assure you, we will influence them! For now, however, let's stick with our scenario of what happens when there is no one to help change minds and influence behavior. In this scenario, we are left on our own, continuing to struggle, paralyzed in this stage, waiting and waiting for something to happen.

The Line in the Sand

Some years ago my wife and I owned a Mercury Marquis that was one interesting piece of work. It was a fine car, but we had it for quite some time, and over the years it developed some rather interesting—shall we say—habits. It had a rattle of some sort in the back wheel, but we got used to it. The dashboard light had a mind of its own and would turn on and off on its own schedule, but we got used to it. It had a ding here, and some rust there, and the mileage wasn't quite what we had hoped, but we got used to all of it. In fact there were a lot of nagging issues with the Gray Ghost, as we called that car, and we mumbled from time to time that we should probably get rid of it, but that was just idle chatter.

Then one day the Gray Ghost surprised us with a new interesting habit. As we were driving to a friend's house in a quiet little suburban neighborhood in Maryland, early in the morning, the horn started honking all by itself. As soon as we completed our turn into the neighborhood the horn stopped. Mortified, we continued on. A couple of blocks later we turned again, and again the horn, apparently with a mind of its own, went off. Quickly, we completed the turn and it stopped again. As luck would have it, we had to make at least four more turns, and each time we took a turn, that horn announced our arrival to everyone on the street.

When we finally reached our friend's house and turned off the car, we were clear on two things. First, we needed to cut the wire to that car horn. Second, we needed to say good-bye to the Gray Ghost. We had crossed that line in the sand from not liking something, to deciding to do something about it. We had made a commitment to change.

✻ ✻ ✻

When it comes to making decisions, it's clear that we go through repeatable, predictable stages. However, within this cycle there is one significant moment of truth that seems to be missed by many, and yet is vital to those who seek to change minds. I call it the line in the sand.

I am not a cynic, but I am a realist. These two things I know to be true:

- It is human nature to spend months, if not years, living with problems we are capable of fixing but don't. We wait until little problems become big problems, and change often comes too late.

- It is human nature to fear change, and that fear can be so blinding that we can't see the size and scope of problems until there is a difficult, if not devastating, occurrence.

We live with these problems, we justify these problems, we whine about these problems, we sulk about these problems, we turn away, and we even deny these problems exist. And then something happens.

That something can be as simple as a comment that catches us by surprise, or as disastrous as being fired from a job. But something happens. When that something happens we cross a line I've nicknamed the *fix, don't fix line* and it is a mythical line in the sand. When we cross the line, we don't commit to a solution; we commit to a change.

- We can complain about an unfulfilling job for years. We've crossed that line in the sand when we redo our resume and begin networking.

- We can complain about an unfulfilling relationship for years. We've crossed that line in the sand when we find ourselves a therapist and set an appointment.

- We can complain about a car that has too many miles on it. We've crossed that line in the sand when we find ourselves pulling into a dealership.

There are moments of truth in all our lives, which frequently initiate change. Personally, I'd rather help someone avoid a catastrophe than clean one up, and that's why this line in the sand is so important to me. Understanding this line reminds me how important it is to help others navigate this line. It's not unusual to struggle with change; we all do. What is unusual is for people, on their own, to fix these problems before it's too late.

THE CRITERIA STAGE

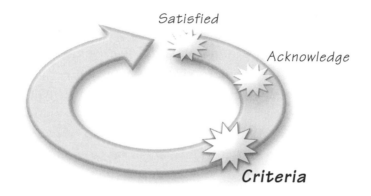

And then something *does* happen. Sometimes it can be a traumatic situation, and other times it can be the combination of a lot of smaller issues. However, one way or another, we make our decision for change and begin to look for alternatives.

The Straw that Broke the Camel's Back

One day, on a beautiful summer evening, we threw a party. Storm windows were down, speakers were on, and sound-a-lizers were sound-a-lizing. Later in the evening, when we heard, "What's that roaring sound?" from a party guest for the third time, my wife and I looked at each other and made a decision. We didn't put our house on the market in the morning, nor did we contact a realtor . . . yet; however, we had crossed a critical decision point. We were committed to making a change. This was our house, but it was on a cul-de-sac that was just too loud with traffic noise, and we were fed up with it.

✳ ✳ ✳

It could be a bad kayaking trip that left a smoker out of breath and fatigued, or it could just as easily be seeing someone else's misfortune. Once the problem grows in size, we look for alternatives. Sadly, often this newfound realization comes too late.

When I sold insurance for New York Life, one thing the managers hated to see was agents sitting by the phone, waiting for it to ring. People do not sit down and call their agents unless something is wrong, usually *very* wrong. On the rare occasions when I did receive a call from a customer looking for insurance, our conversation would literally go like this:

"Hi, I'm looking for insurance."
"That's wonderful. What did the doctor tell you?"
"Pardon?"
"Well, when you went to the doctor today, what did he tell you?"
"Uh, well . . . he said my blood pressure was going up."

Our problems dominate the size and shape of our needs.

I wasn't a genius or a palm reader. I just understood human nature. In this stage of our decision making, we have often gone through an emotional crisis of some sort and are looking to fix whatever is bothering us. The single most critical lesson to learn within the process lies right here. It is proved over and over again, day after day, that our problems clearly shape our needs. Consider some of the decisions you've made in the past.

- That house you bought a few years ago just had to have a fenced-in yard. I'm wondering how many times your dog got loose from your previous, unfenced yard.

- That job you took a few years ago just had to be within ten miles of your home. I'm wondering how many hours you spent snarled in traffic during the difficult commute you used to have.

- That car you bought a few years ago just had to have Bluetooth installed. I'm wondering how close you were to rear-ending the car in front of you while trying to dial a number on your cell phone.

- That employee you hired a few years ago just had to have a track record of loyalty and cooperation. I'm wondering how undependable the employee you replaced was, and how damaging his or her lack of loyalty was.

The Problem Shapes the Need

No, we didn't go looking for a realtor the day after that infamous party; we waited about a week. The market had changed to a buyer's market, which meant we had a lot of houses to choose from. Big ones, small ones, simple ones, fancy ones, and yet, we were fixated on only one criterion: a quiet location.

This fixation led us to the quietest location in the Washington metropolitan area—Great Falls, Virginia. With most of the city still bound by two-acre zoning laws, and only one two-lane road that ran through it, we had found our quiet town. This was by no means a coincidence. This was going to be our new house, perhaps on a cul-de-sac, but without traffic noise, and we were excited about it.

No, needs don't just pop up out of nowhere, nor does our motivation to seek change. Now, with a better understanding of not just *what* we need but also of how our problems *become* needs, we move to the next stage.

THE INVESTIGATE STAGE

We now look for a solution. Equipped with a list of criteria, the search for a resolution begins. The *investigate*

stage may involve the act of actually looking for the same product at different locations. For example, if you were choosing a car, you may decide to buy a Ford Taurus. Then the second half of your decision would be where to buy it. Chances are you might visit a couple of dealerships in search of your dream Ford.

The Search for Silence

We were so fixated on the quiet location of this house, we actually put each house we viewed through the, "sound test." We never visited a home during rush hour, and when we drove up to it, we would roll down all the windows and shut off our car engine, and if we heard anything that sounded remotely like another car, we did not even enter the house. Any noise was a deal breaker. After all, this was going to be our new house, perhaps on a cul-de-sac, but one without traffic noise, and we would not compromise.

* * *

Some of the individuals whose decisions I have tracked and studied have proudly told me, "I went with the first car or house I saw." I believe this assertion but I question its logic. Having learned my own lessons, this is not something I would brag about. Often, even if the first selection turns out to be the best selection, the more thorough we are in the investigate stage, the less buyer's remorse we are likely to experience down the road.

With the comparing and shopping out of the way, we have finished our homework. At last, we are nearly ready to make the final decision.

THE SELECT STAGE

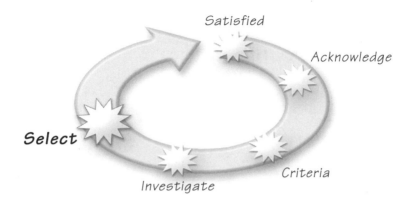

And all that is left to do now is make your move. Perhaps as a result of the slow, sometimes painful, process to get here, it is not unusual to feel a sense of euphoria when you say yes and act on the urge to change. When you actually study how people make choices, you observe that their final decision is often the easiest one. They often feel a release of tension when they make their ultimate decision.

Pulling the Trigger

After a few months of careful searching, we took the plunge and bought our new house. We finally found a home, on a meticulously noise-tested cul-de-sac, and we loved it!

✳ ✳ ✳

There really is not that much more that can be said about the *select stage*. It might just represent the most basic, quickest step within the cycle. Unfortunately, you better not blink, because chances are you will not stay here for long. Often, within months, we move on.

THE RECONSIDER STAGE

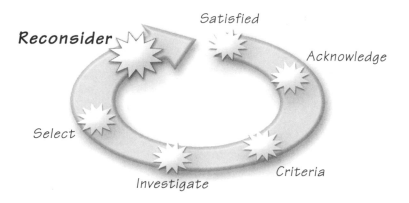

Now we head toward the *reconsider stage*. Sometimes referred to as buyer's remorse, this stage is inevitable. It's really not a question of *if* we go through this stage; it's more a question of *when*.

The severity of the reconsider stage is often in direct proportion to the size of the commitment of the solution. After a brief touch of remorse, we move on through the cycle, landing in the satisfied stage, and the process begins to repeat itself once again.

Buyer's Remorse

Buying a house is a big deal, and I'm not going to tell you I didn't have a second thought or two the first time I heard a slight groan from the plumbing, but it was our house, on a meticulously noise-tested cul-de-sac, and we loved it!

With a few variations, this *repeatable* and *predictable* process is the same from decision to decision, scenario to scenario, and industry to industry. Therefore, success is not solely determined by your ability to apply a series of tactics used to change minds and influence behavior. In fact, success lies in your ability to understand where someone is in his or her decision cycle and to line up the appropriate tactics necessary to influence change. Of course, this is a fluid process and it is important to remember that the process doesn't end here.

The Process Continues

It's been twenty-two years since we moved into our home in Great Falls, Virginia. We raised three wonderful children in this quiet home, on a cul-de-sac, and we have loved it. We're approaching our next phase in life as empty nesters, and that means another move. We got our quiet home in a fairly rural location. Of course, to have a quiet location, you have to sacrifice other things. A fairly rural location means limited mass transit opportunities, and a lot of driving for even the most basic needs. It also means frequent loss of power from downed trees during even a moderate storm. So, our next house may very well be in the city, where we can use mass transit, and wake up and walk for a cup of coffee. There's a very good chance our house will have a generator as well. I'm sure it will be a beautiful house, perhaps on a cul-de-sac, and I'm quite sure we'll love it. . . .

✻ ✻ ✻

Over the past twenty years I have continued to poll my audiences in a participant pool that now numbers well over 100,000. Through good times, and bad, strong economies and weak, tangible and intangible solutions, the numbers have not varied by more than two percentage points. Three statistics should jump off this chart:

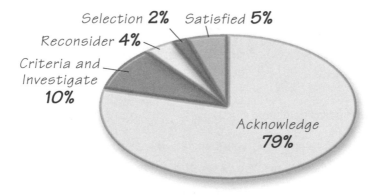

Credit: Jolles Associates, Inc.

1. 79 percent of those polled, when not pressured to consider a solution—that's almost eight out of ten—will admit to an awareness of a problem. Unfortunately, these same people will also admit to not wanting to fix the problem . . . yet.

2. 10 percent of those polled are considering alternatives to their current problem and are receptive to a solution if one is offered.

3. 5 percent of those polled are in fact completely satisfied with their current situation. (If you are struggling with that number, and feel it's just too low for you to believe, I ask you to suspend your disbelief for a chapter and I'll be happy to tell you exactly why so many people deny having problems.)

It's referred to as the *decision cycle* for a reason. The cycle is fluid and continuous. Understanding this cycle of change provides a key building block when learning *how to change minds,* because understanding this part of the process provides logic to the moves we must learn to make when influencing behavior. It also reminds me of an important question you will find repeated in the text that follows, the first question we must ask ourselves before we make even one strategic move, "Where is this person within his or her decision cycle?"

3

Establishing Trust

Those who manipulate *don't ask for trust.*

Those who influence *don't need to ask for trust; they earn it.*

It all begins with trust. Nothing else really matters, nor will any other tactics that are taught really matter, if there isn't trust. Can the art of creating trust be learned? Yes. Is there a process that can be defined for creating trust? Yes.

THE OLDEST LESSON IN TRUST

For over twenty years, I have been marching into training rooms all over the world, asking audiences to help me figure out what makes people trust other people. I word the question this way:

> I want you to think of someone you trust or have trusted in the past on a very deep level. This could be a parent, a teacher, a colleague, a manager, or anyone else you can think of. Start by telling me how this person makes you feel.

Typical responses include:

- He makes me feel important.
- She makes me feel intelligent.
- He makes me feel as if he cares about me.
- She makes me feel as if she is interested in what I'm saying.

All good responses. The next question I ask is this: "Now tell me a little more about the person you are describing."

- She is honest.
- He is empathetic.
- She is interesting.
- He seems to know what he is talking about.

Again, terrific responses. Then comes the best part. I follow up with one more question. It's a simple little question, but the response never ceases to amaze me: "Tell me what they are actually *doing* that makes you trust them so much." Things get awfully quiet when I ask that question. People seem almost dumbfounded, if not exasperated, often repeating what they have already told me. "Uh, they just seem like they can be trusted!"

The irony is, I've watched for decades as people struggle to answer this question, and yet what they are searching for is not only a simple answer, it's something that almost everyone has learned at some point in his or her life. Unfortunately, although we all may have learned it, we seem to have systematically forgotten it. So what does everyone learn but quickly forget? You want to create trust? Ask questions, and then listen.

My Father-in-Law

I'll never forget the first time I met my future wife Ronni's father. I was understandably nervous, but Ronni kept insisting, "You'll like him. Everyone likes him." Everyone likes him? Perhaps, but this did little to ease my apprehension.

Then came the big meeting. He warmly shook my hand, and we began to speak. To my surprise, it was one of the easiest conversations I had ever had with a person I had never met. I looked up at the clock and couldn't believe we had been speaking, freely and effortlessly, for over thirty minutes. I was elated, and told Ronni, "Boy, you weren't kidding, I really like him! He's so easy to talk with!" She nodded her head and smiled.

A few weeks later, I met Ronni's father again, and once again was astonished at how easily the conversation seemed to flow. I could spend all day talking to this man! Once again I told Ronni, "I love talking to your dad!" This time I looked a little more carefully at her reaction and saw her slightly roll her eyes when I reacted the way I did.

When I questioned her about her reaction she smiled and said, "I know you like my dad; everyone likes my dad. Do you know why you like my dad so much? Because he never speaks. He asks questions, and he listens to the answers." That was the first time it dawned on me that throughout our conversations, these conversations I enjoyed so much, he never told me a thing about himself. He dialed his questions into me. Not only did these questions make me like him, they made me trust him.

✳ ✳ ✳

We communicate in three ways: We listen, we ask questions, or we make statements. I believe that asking questions and listening are the driving forces behind that trusted person list you just looked at. And we can thank Xerox for taking this hunch of mine and proving that it's a fact. About a decade ago, Xerox sent out over 5,000 surveys to its clientele and posed this simple question:

> Given the fact that there are only three ways we can communicate with you, would you please rank these three types of communication regarding how you want us to communicate with you?

The answers that came out of this survey were staggering. Not only did asking questions and listening come in at almost a dead heat as the number one answer, what was truly amazing was what happened to the response, "making statements." It was nonexistent! It fell off the radar. No one selected it as his or her number one response. Does that really surprise you? When asked how he wants to be communicated with, who in his right mind would respond, "I want someone to create trust with me by meeting me and then telling me all about himself!"

The more the people you are communicating with talk, the more they like the person they are talking to.

If this is so obvious, why do so few people ask questions and listen? There are a few theories out there, but I'm going to tell you what I think is the biggest culprit. You might not like it because the answer may be peering at you from your mirror. It involves our thirst for knowledge.

THE BATTLE FOR KNOWLEDGE

If you ever want to start an argument with another person, particularly someone who prides himself on his wise thoughts, tell him you feel knowledge is overrated. This comment drives self-proclaimed wise people crazy!

When you stop and think about it, many of us have invested a lot in the pursuit of knowledge. It begins with our first trip to nursery school, and progresses through elementary, middle, and high school. For many it continues into college with the pursuit of an undergraduate degree, a master's, and sometimes even a doctorate. Doctors learn to heal, accountants learn to balance numbers, lawyers learn to interpret the law; the list goes on and on.

Then we go to work, and the first thing most of us experience is the pursuit of knowledge of an entirely new kind, one based on the specific requirements of our job. Many occupations require a constant upgrade in our job knowledge through continuing education requirements. The accumulation of all this knowledge takes years of dedication.

That's why educated people often take exception to a simple statement I make when conducting workshops: "Knowledge? It's overrated."

Before you, too, throw up your hands and roll your eyes, I want you to think for a moment about those who have earned your trust, and whom you deeply respect as communicators. Did they earn this lofty status by their display of intelligence, or did they earn it through their ability to make you believe that their actions were in your best interests? I'm guessing these people you trust and respect knew how to ask questions and listen.

Think about the last time you were led to believe in a solution because you felt comfortable with the person you were communicating with. Did he or she earn this level of trust by bowling you over with knowledge, or was it by asking questions and listening?

I am not asserting that knowledge is not a necessary part of who we are. What I am saying is a lot of smart people in this world struggle mightily with their ability to get people to believe in them. What I am saying is that knowledge is necessary; it's just a bit overrated.

It was either Albert Einstein or I who once said, "Imagination is more important than knowledge." (I'm pretty sure it was Einstein.)

THE SECOND OLDEST LESSON IN TRUST

We now know for a fact that we create trust and lay the groundwork for influence by asking questions and listening. But how many questions do we ask? What types of questions do we ask? Let me introduce you to the second oldest lesson in trust: You must learn the difference between an *open* question and a *closed* question. Let's start with a quick definition.

An open question is simply a question that cannot be answered with a yes or a no. Open questions

- Get people talking.

- Open up people who are a little more reserved.

Start your questions with words like the ones you see below, and your questions will be open:

| What | When | Describe |
| Why | Where | Tell |

A closed question is a question that can be answered with a yes or a no. Closed questions are not necessarily bad questions to ask, but not now, and not when you are trying to establish trust. Closed questions

- Can shut down a talkative person.

- Confirm or test information.

Start your questions with words like the ones you see below, and your questions will be closed.

| Are | Will | Can |
| Would | If | Did |

It's not an interrogation; it's a conversation.

Sometimes, when using these probes, you have to be careful not to pump your questions out too quickly. And do not overuse closed questions. Watch a good court trial someday, and you will know what I mean. By avoiding closed questions, you will reduce your chances of "leading the witnesses."

I'm about ready to leave these two classic ideas behind, but not without a commitment from you. Here's what I'm asking you to do. Carefully read the short declaration on this page. If you do agree with it, then commit yourself to it. And if you do, you'll have taken one of the most important steps in learning not only how to establish trust, but also how to influence behavior.

A Declaration

> From now on, when I enter into a conversation with someone I'm looking to establish trust with, I will not only lead with questions, I'll try to ask open questions.
>
> Signed: _____

People aren't going to remember what you said, or what you did. In the end, people are going to remember how you made them feel.

IF YOU REMEMBER NOTHING ELSE

Imagine for a moment you were attending a program I was delivering and you heard me say,

If you remember nothing else from the hours or days we spend together, I ask that, whenever in your life you are communicating with another individual and attempting to influence his or her actions, you commit yourself to asking questions and listening. If you do this, this will be the most valuable workshop you will ever have attended in your life.

Of course I follow this up with a reminder that we are just scratching the surface of influence, and new and wonderful lessons are about to come. However, I mean what I say. If you remember these first two lessons—(1) to ask questions and listen, and (2) to understand the difference between an open and closed question—the results will have a profound effect on your life.

THE FOUR A'S OF TRUST

Now that you have the two oldest lessons under your belt, let's start working on some new ones. But before we do, I think it's important to tell you that as simple as they may appear, they are often overlooked. Don't believe me? I was part of a pretty high-powered think tank that did an amazing job of missing these critical lessons.

Without trust, there is no influence

I remember well the first sales process I ever helped to create. We threw everything but the kitchen sink into this process. Yes, sir, we were going to leave nothing to chance, and the sixteen-step process we created would prove that every tactic involved in selling was in this process. What I realized later was that we were *almost* right. Every tactic involved in selling was in the process except the most important one: attention to trust.

Oh, we talked about trust, and we told stories about trust; however, we didn't apply one repeatable, predictable step to the process we were working on that actually *taught* trust. In our defense, we felt that trust was a given; we felt it was obvious; we felt it was somehow intuitive.

How wrong we were. We built an amazing process that spelled out every move a person could make other than the first move to be made. Sadly, without trust, the rest of the process becomes anemic. We went back and performed our own version of a retrofit to the process, but I still think back with amazement on how we could have missed it. How could we have assumed trust is easily earned, and intuitive? Without trust there can be no influence.

Correcting that mistake has become a twenty-year passion, so let's correct it here and now. Keep these "four A's" in mind, and you'll be on your way not only to creating trust, but also to influencing behavior.

CASE STUDY

As we look into the various processes that involve change, I believe it's easier to understand the steps by providing case studies, and tracking the relevant responses. That said, here is your first case study.

THE CASE OF THE MISGUIDED MOTORCYCLE RIDER

The Art of Trust

Background: Your spouse loves that motorcycle, and you've been trying to get that motorcycle retired for years.

Tactic: The words of a friend keep ringing in your ears: "There are two types of motorcycle riders—them who have been down, and them who are going down." You would desperately like to change the mind of your spouse and influence the retirement of that motorcycle, but so far the conversations have ended in frustration and anger.

ASK OPEN QUESTIONS

I'll bet you saw that one coming, but I can't tell you how often I work with people who treat a conversation like a game of Twenty Questions. I've given you the reasons for asking these questions, as well as how to ask them. It's all about trust now, so make no mistake about it, here's one of the most important times to keep your questions open.

The Best Question I Ever Heard

I recently had a conversation with my buddy Bubba, a salesman I've known for over twenty years. He is one of the best salesmen I've ever met. We were talking about questions that help build trust between people and allow us to learn volumes about another person. He shared the best question I've ever come across.

We know that if we are going to use questions to create trust, the initial questions are critical. That's why the simplicity and effectiveness of the following question resonated so deeply within me. The question was this: "Everyone has a story. What's yours?"

You would be amazed where this question can lead. The answer can provide an instant window into another person's personality, just by the depth of his or her response. The answer can provide information that someone may rarely tell another individual. The truth is that people *want* to tell their stories. The question is completely nonthreatening; people can answer with as much or as little depth as makes them comfortable.

The next time you are in a situation where you really want to get to know another person, and you want to begin to create trust, ask that question. Then settle back, and listen carefully. There's no telling where the story might end up, but the conversation will end in a deeper level of trust.

※ ※ ※

ACTIVELY LISTEN

So you are now prepared to *ask* open questions. The problem is, this first tip doesn't mean a thing if you don't listen to the response. And don't just listen (as in not being the one doing the talking); truly, actively listen!

I'm not talking about blankly nodding along, prematurely offering solutions, fidgeting, doodling, texting, contradicting, or looking at your watch. I'm talking about making eye contact, focusing, taking notes, dialing in, and really listening.

Franklin Delano Roosevelt found the polite small talk of social functions at the White House somewhat tedious. He maintained that those present on such occasions rarely paid much attention to what was said to them. To illustrate the point, he would sometimes amuse himself by greeting guests with the words, "I murdered my grandmother this morning." The response was invariably one of polite approval. On one occasion, however, the president happened upon an attentive listener. On hearing Roosevelt's outrageous remark, the guest replied diplomatically, "I'm sure she had it coming to her."

Like so many people, I struggle with being a better listener. I try, I really do. I've read about being a better listener, I've attended seminars about being a better listener, I've written about being a better listener, and I've even put a module in two of my training programs, which means (gasp) I've even taught people how to be better listeners. So, at the risk of appearing slightly hypocritical, let me take an unconventional approach to trying to solve this problem.

Rather than join the masses and tell you what you need to do to improve your listening, I'd like to take a contrarian view of this issue, and tell you what *not* to do to improve your listening. Some years ago I attended a listening seminar and was intrigued when presented with a list of habits to avoid. I liked this angle, and felt I could certainly identify with it, so I set out creating my own survey. For over a year I polled my seminar audiences about the most annoying listening habits they observed in others. Here are the top ten answers I received.

They

1. Interrupt me.

2. Make no eye contact.

3. Check email or text messages.

4. Jump in as if to make their point before I'm finished making mine.

5. Appear distracted or uninterested.

6. Show no expression.

7. Turn everything I say into a story involving them.

8. Look at their watch while I'm speaking.

9. Ask a question to which I have just given the answer.

10. Visually drift off, looking and studying things around them instead of looking at me.

I've always liked this list because in a sense, by learning what annoys others, we get a blueprint of good listening habits we should try to incorporate.

Listening is crucial—and I mean complete, undivided listening. It's hard to do. What's more, contrary to popular belief, in no way is it an instinctive behavior; it requires mental discipline that rivals some of the most challenging behaviors we've attempted to master. But the results are amazing.

AIM YOUR QUESTIONS

When you set out to influence behavior, you need to begin by figuring out what your ultimate goal is. It sounds easy, but don't be deceived. I think it's one of the most challenging aspects of learning to influence behavior. When I refer to aiming your question, I don't mean standard rapport-building questions such as, How are you doing today? and Did you see the ball game last night?

Let the other person paint the picture.

I'm not saying you won't build rapport with aimed questions; I am saying there's a lot more involved in asking them. Remember, we are not just establishing trust here; we are laying the foundation for change. When you learn to *aim* your questions, you need to have a goal, or an end, in mind toward which to move your conversation.

IT BEGINS WITH KNOWING WHAT YOU'RE AIMING AT

Through the years I've conducted workshops for many different companies, but one of my favorites has been Toyota. I'll never forget the first time I met this client. I was summoned to a meeting with high-level Toyota executives at Toyota University in California. Toyota was trying to determine which of a handful of vendors would conduct their training.

I don't often feel intimidated walking into a room, but that day I did. I began to talk about the art of influence, and made the point that questions needed to be aimed, and that the aiming of these questions begins with a clear understanding of the conversation's goal. I inadvertently asked a question that seemed both to stump them and to bother them. I asked, "Given the fact that there are many cars on the road, in a perfect world, what do you want potential customers to want when they walk onto your showroom floor?"

The room grew eerily quiet. I stammered a bit, and followed my question with, "Well, I'm asking because I can't begin the process of influence until I know clearly what I want the solution to be." More blank stares, until finally one of the most senior people in the room spoke up and said, "Could you please give us a few minutes to provide you with a response to your question?"

I was then led out of the room a bit disheartened, thinking I had blown my opportunity to work with such a wonderful client. A few minutes later they called me back in. When I walked into the room I was handed a small piece of paper. On it were three clear strengths that were unique to Toyota as a manufacturer. I looked up, smiled, and said, "Perfect. Does anyone else know what's on this piece of paper?" The group collectively shook their heads, and I said, "Well, that's where we would begin."

Two days later they awarded me with a contract, and I've maintained a relationship with Toyota ever since.

AVOID PROBLEMS

Who wants to admit to a problem they have no intention of fixing? Learning to avoid problems early in the conversation provides us with an explanation as to why so many people will deny they have a problem to begin with. Imagine if you were trying to create trust in a conversation regarding the motorcycle case study, and you asked a question like this: "Do you have concerns about riding your motorcycle?"

Such a question sets the mind of the person you are trying to influence racing, and what's going through it sounds something like this:

> Do I have concerns about riding my motorcycle?
> Let's see. If I answer that question yes, there will be no getting out of this conversation. If I answer that question yes, I will probably have to commit to something. Heck, I'm not sure if I have concerns or not, but I don't want to get rid of my bike, so I know one thing for sure—I'm not admitting anything right now!

The answer you hear is a simple no, which will probably be followed up with an excuse or a lie as to why he or she doesn't want to make a change. What's worse, *you* are the one who initiated that lie.

You have probably told quite a number of these little lies yourself. The art of working within this stage involves getting a person to trust you. Avoiding that person's problems in the beginning can go a long way toward earning the trust that you will need if you wish to influence a change.

There is a process for trust. It requires the blending of old lessons with a few more detailed reminders: (1) ask open questions, (2) actively listen, (3) aim your questions, and (4) avoid problems. It's not a perfect science, but each of these steps represents critical reminders.

THE CASE OF THE MISGUIDED MOTORCYCLE RIDER

Applying the Four A's of Trust

The Need: You want to create trust with the person you are communicating with.

The Tactic: You create trust by *asking* open questions, *aiming* those questions to a particular strength of your solution, *avoiding* problems, and *actively* listening.

The Examples:

"What type of roads do you typically ride on?"

"What kind of weather conditions do you typically ride in?"

So our journey continues. Without a foundation of *believing* in what you are about to influence someone else to do, there is nothing to build on. Without understanding the process people go through when they make decisions, there is no logic to the tactics you use. Without trust, there is no climate in which to change another person's mind. Now it's time to continue our journey, to add the steps necessary to create the most difficult move of all. It's time to create *urgency*.

4

The Blueprint for Changing Minds

Those who manipulate *put their faith in the right argument.*

Those who influence *put their faith in the right question.*

Influence may begin with trust, but it can go nowhere without urgency. To learn the art of influence, you must learn the art of *urgency*. Remember that fifteen years of research tells us that eight out of ten people are aware they have an issue but they just don't want to do anything about it. Well, I'm only allowed to say this once, so I'll say it now: If you master any techniques from this book, master the techniques taught in this chapter. Clearly, I'm setting you up for the most important part of the process here, and yet, as important as I feel these tactics are, that doesn't mean these tactics don't elicit some emotional feelings. If ever there was a spotlight on the precarious line between *influence* and *manipulation,* it sits right here.

Please Welcome . . . the Scab Picker

Some years ago I was sitting in a green room, getting ready to speak at a financial conference. Another speaker was on stage, and he began to speak less than glowingly about me. Then I heard these immortal words: "Today we're going to hear from someone I call a scab picker—a man who believes that you must continue to ask people about their pain!" A few minutes later I took to the stage, grabbed the microphone, and introduced myself.

> Ladies and gentlemen, my name is Rob Jolles, and I am a scab picker. I consider the greatest act of compassion one human being can extend to another is to move someone past fear of change, and help him or her avoid the tragedy of procrastination. I do this through the act of questioning, to create a sense of urgency in an empathetic, and honest, manner. And I'm proud of it.

✳ ✳ ✳

If people are so intelligent and know fully about their problems, how come they take so long to do anything about them?

We have come to a crossroad. Those who can move individuals from understanding they have a problem to actually wanting to do something about their problem can *influence*. Those who cannot may be successful at some things but will struggle when put in a position that requires the skills to influence. I may be a bit biased, but I'm not sure I can come up with a role in life that does not require some ability to influence. It is no coincidence that this part of learning *the art of influencing without manipulation* is the most challenging. However, if you need a little influence yourself, I believe learning to do this will serve you well for the rest of your life.

THE CASE OF THE FINANCIAL HOBBY

The Blueprint for Changing Minds

Background: You are a financial analyst who has met with a particular client twice now. Both meetings seemed to go well, but ended with, "Let me think about it." Your client treats his financial planning more like a hobby than the potential life-changing event you feel it has the long-term potential to be. He has dreams of retirement and the responsibilities of three kids' educations, yet he has met every solution you offer him with procrastination.

Change Needed: You want to get him over his fear of change, and create urgency regarding his financial picture. You know all too well that the path he is on, chasing stocks and following various fads, will end in disaster. Today you want to change his *mind*.

If you study this chapter carefully, and immediately try to practice what you have learned, you will succeed. When you learn to create trust, you learn to avoid problems at all costs. When you learn to create urgency, quite the opposite is true. You've earned the right to enter into a conversation about someone else's problems. Now all you have to do is convince him or her to make a change.

Those who manipulate *tell others about their problems.*

Those who influence *allow others to tell them about their problems.*

There *is* a repeatable, predictable approach to creating urgency. It should come as no surprise that this process involves questions, lots of questions. As a matter of fact, it requires a sequence of questions that fit into three simple steps, which I'll delineate now.

Step 1: Identify the problem

I refer to these questions as *identifying probes* because that's what needs to happen first. Until someone understands or admits he or she has a particular problem, there is no logic in working to solve it. This can be difficult. Most people will resist admitting to others they have a problem—*especially* when they think that their problem is mild. If they do admit to having a problem, they often fear they will somehow have to commit themselves to doing something about it.

However, once there is trust, if there is a problem, people will not hesitate as much to admit it. The problem is, they often do not understand how severe the issue may be or has the potential to be. Many will not admit to the size of a problem simply because they have never sat down and carefully analyzed it.

THE CASE OF THE FINANCIAL HOBBY

Identifying Probes

The Need: You have created trust and need to have the person you are influencing acknowledge there is a potential problem.

The Tactic: You want to move from the trust-based questions you have used thus far to the problem-based questions found in the *identifying probes*.

The Examples: "What challenges have you experienced with some of the more aggressive moves you've made in the market?"

or

"What kinds of concerns do you have regarding the lack of time you have to fully investigate some of the decisions you have been making?"

Once again, it is critical for you to use open questions. You are beginning to tread on sacred ground here, and you definitely do not want to be perceived as pushy.

"I object, your Honor; leading the witness!"

If you ever want to see the two concepts—easing into identifying probes, and the importance of asking open questions—watch a good trial lawyer in action. This lawyer will not step up to cross-examine a witness by jumping directly into the issues at hand. She will strategically lay out many questions to ease into the issues. However, even after she's into these issues, you won't hear questions like, "Isn't it a fact you were irresponsible?" or "Wouldn't you agree that you were irresponsible and negligent?" Such questions will be met with a robust, "I object, your Honor! She's leading the witness!"

An objection like this is often sustained, and the questions must be rephrased. "Mr. Johnson, would you please explain exactly what you did once you entered the house?"

The irony is the objecting lawyer is in fact helping the opponent by reminding her to open up her questions whereby a lot more information can be ascertained and a witness can wander into areas he or she had not been prepared to discuss if this happens.

If you can keep your questions open, there's a good chance you'll get ·the conversation started in the right direction. However, there's another problem you must avoid, and that's saying the word "problem." People seem to really hate that word. Do you have a *problem* with that?

Here are some words that you can substitute for the word "problem":

- Concern
- Difficulty
- Dissatisfaction

- Challenge
- Barrier
- Limitation

- Obstacle
- Trouble
- Issue

These words will swap nicely for the word "problem" and allow you to get the person you are conversing with to *identify* or admit he or she has a problem. Sometimes, people need just one more little push.

Those who manipulate *"push" a person through his statements, telling him about a problem that may exist.*

Those who influence *"push" a person through his questions, allowing that person to discover the potential of a problem that may exist.*

This "little push" involves spelling out more of the problem than I would prefer, but sometimes it is necessary. Some people would rather not deal with a particular issue or problem until it actually occurs. It is not a reflection of stubbornness to procrastinate and avoid the thought of serious problems. It is human nature. The words you are looking for are, "What happens if . . . ?"

★ THE CASE OF THE FINANCIAL HOBBY

What Happens If . . . ?

The Need: You want to move the conversation to a problem that has the potential to occur.

The Examples: *"What challenges have you experienced with some of the more aggressive moves you've made in the market?"*

- "None; I haven't really been burned by any decision I've made up to this point."

- *"What happens if one of these products does blow up on you?"*

- "Uh, well, that would be an issue because I'm counting on these funds, but, well, uh. . . ."

WAITING FOR THE PHONE TO RING

As a life insurance salesman, my phone rang exactly twice in close to three years of selling. The first time it rang I was thrilled! The second time it rang, I responded by asking, "What did the doctor tell you *today?*"

It doesn't take a genius to apply influence to another who is looking for change whose *what if* has become a *what is*. It takes someone who is skilled in influence. You could certainly ask someone what concerns she has about her health, but don't be surprised to hear, "I have no concerns; I'm as healthy as a horse!" That's when a simple, "What happens if?" does the trick.

Now we have ourselves a problem to work with. Watch the temptation to overuse the phrase "What happens if?" because you don't want all your questions to start sounding the same. The irony is that it's often the *what if* that truly saves another individual.

The intent of learning to influence is to protect someone from what if, *not* what is.

Okay, so now we have identified a concern in the mind of the person we are looking to influence. Where do we go from here? Well, I can tell you where 99 percent of people in this same position would go from here. Right to a solution:

> Client: Uh, well, that would be an issue because I'm counting on these funds, but, well, uh, I mean it isn't my entire nest egg.

> Financial Analyst: Well, if we work together, one of the first things I think you'll appreciate is the asset allocation models that we use. What that does is allow us to balance your portfolio while at the same time key into market leaders who traditionally. . . .

And so on. This probably looks like a familiar conversation to you if you work in the financial industry. It may also look familiar to you if you work with professionals within this industry. It may be familiar, but I can assure you that it's useless.

The real problem is that whatever is concerning the person you are looking to influence does not concern him or her enough. The enticement to launch into a solution tempts those who try to influence the way a mouse is tempted by cheese in a mousetrap. Neither scenario tends to end well.

In fact, attempting to provide a solution, or fixing someone's problem here, often results in a lack of urgency by those being influenced. If there is an actual monetary price involved in the decision, it's not uncommon for price to dominate our decision-making. However, the truth is, there is always a price to be paid for living with problems and not addressing them. The price paid in our financial example may be a life-changing experience for other family members involved, and a potential nasty spiral for a husband and wife. One final price to be paid when there is no urgency is for the possibility for change to be lost in a sea of procrastination. Fortunately, the next step of the process addresses this very point.

Step 2: Develop the problem

It is not easy, and not instinctive, and, sadly for many, any opportunity to influence is lost right here. Your temptation is to move on. To influence, you must stay put. You need to ask more questions—questions that go deeper. I refer to these questions as *developing probes* because, quite simply, you *must* develop the problem more. The way you develop a problem is to continue to ask questions about it.

Often, people do not want to talk much about their concerns. If I'm there to influence, I *do*. People will avoid thinking about the long-term effects a particular problem might have. If I'm there to influence, I *won't*. People shy away from contemplating "what if." If I'm there to influence, that is precisely what I *will* do! After a person has experienced a major problem, there is no longer a need for influence. It's too late to help. Sadly, the only thing you can do now is help pick up the pieces.

The art of using developing probes boils down to this: You have to be more curious with those you are looking to influence. Once the problem has been defined, stop allowing those you are looking to influence to run away from it! Stay put. Stay curious.

THE CASE OF THE FINANCIAL HOBBY

Developing Probes

The Need: You have *identified* the problem with the person you are influencing. Now it's time to study the problem further.

The Tactic: *Developing probes* are needed to get this person to see the size and scope of the problem.

"What challenges have you experienced with some of the more aggressive moves you've made in the market?"

The Examples: "How much have you lost up to this point?"

"What had you intended to use that money for?"

"And?"

Key words used in developing probes are not quite as simple to track as the other probes because the art of using developing probes requires extending the conversation and is not necessarily triggered by one specific word. Remember, you are simply trying to extend the conversation.

When in Doubt, Throw an "And?" Out

I learned a wonderful lesson from a student I was working with in Birmingham, Alabama, on how to use developing probes. After I completed the program, he offered me a lift to the airport, and during our drive, he shocked me with his simple lesson. He was quite courteous as he expressed his gratitude for what I had taught him and told me this story.

> You know, before you came to town I used my own method. It's probably not as good as yours, but it sure is easy. As a matter of fact, it has only one step to it. You see, when I'm in the bank and someone tells me they have a problem, I just say, "And?"

※ ※ ※

I am not saying the "And?" method is right for everyone, but it does have a place in my world of influence. If you are having difficulty using developing probes, you might want to remember our friend from Birmingham who used the simplest developing probe I've ever heard of. Here are some other words that might be of use from time to time:

- React
- Link
- And

- Respond
- Relate
- Tell me more

- Feel
- Think
- Reply

We can wait for a problem to devastate someone, or we can have a conversation about it.

Make no mistake—these probes can be disturbing. In a sense, a problem exists symbolically as a wound exists. The more pain the wound creates, the closer a person is to doing something about it. If you want to influence behavior, I implore you not to rush in to put a Band-Aid on this wound. Avoiding the more difficult questions and telling someone what to do about his or her problem does just that.

To me, the art of influence can be compared with a good professional fight. (I'll find a kinder, gentler analogy to work with in a moment, but stick with me for now.) Think about what happens in the first couple of rounds of a fight between two respectable fighters. As a fight fan, I can tell you in one word: nothing. In fight terms, the first round is often referred to as a "feeling-out round." The idea is to study your opponent and to try to identify your best fighting strategy.

Consider what happens early on when you are attempting to influence. Your initial trust-based questions represent that feeling-out round. It also provides an opportunity to identify your best influencing strategy, providing a gauge regarding where to throw your punches—and how.

After a couple of rounds in a professional fight, it is not uncommon to hear a corner man tell his fighter, "It's time to throw punches with *bad* intentions!" This tells the fighter basically to take what he has learned and fire some more meaningful punches, which will definitely get the opponent's attention.

When you are attempting to influence another person, that is exactly what you are doing. It is time for you to throw your *probes* with bad intentions. That is where the initial identification probes come in. These questions are not as easy to answer, and often disturb the person you are looking to influence, but they will definitely grab the person's attention.

Now, our boxers teach us another critical lesson. Think about what happens when a good boxer actually lands a solid blow and hurts the opponent. Sometimes, it even cuts the opponent a little bit. I have never heard a boxer say, "Gee, I'm sorry. I seem to have cut your eye a little bit. I'll aim for the other eye." I have never heard the boxer's corner team working with the fighter who has landed the punch call out, "Leave him alone! Stay away from the cut!" In the fights I have seen what is communicated has been quite the opposite: "Stay on him! Don't let him breathe! The cut! Go for the cut!"

When the person you are attempting to influence admits to a problem, you too must "go for the cut." This is no time to be squeamish. Remember, you are frequently dealing with a person who has put off change, so she will wait and wait until the problem she has been avoiding blows up. Often, by then it is too late. If you believe in what you are influencing, you *must* not be afraid to ask the more difficult questions.

One of my mentors in learning how to influence was my dear friend Larry Domonkos. Larry once gave me this little pearl of wisdom as it relates to customers. He said, "Jolles, if they cry, they'll buy!"

I know that I may have offended some of you who are reading this, but it goes to an important point that needs to be made, so hang in there. I can assure you that I fully intend to illustrate this point in a more positive light. However, before I do, let me take this point one step further in the final step of this process.

Step 3: Determine the impact of the problem

So here we are. The person you are looking to influence has seen his predicament methodically expanded using developing probes that better illustrate the potential, true size of the problem. Now it's time for one last question.

These questions allow the person you are influencing to reflect on the big picture involving his problems. In short, the identifying probes allow someone to recognize he has a problem, the developing probes allow someone to understand the potential of the problem, and now the *impact probes* will allow someone to understand the ultimate consequences of the problem. Here are some key words to focus on when using impact probes:

- Consequences
- Impact
- Ramifications

- Repercussions
- Results
- Effects

- Outcome
- Backlash
- Implication

You may find some of the questions I'm suggesting a little over the top. You have your own style and can adapt these questions, but don't forget that until someone decides to "fix" an existing problem, whatever solution you have up your sleeve will be of little interest.

Those who manipulate *passionately explain the impact of not acting on their recommendation.*

Those who influence *compassionately listen to another person explain in his or her own words the impact of not acting to solve an existing problem.*

It can be painful to assist someone to look at the potential ramifications of his or her problems. I am empathetic to this dilemma. It is human nature just to roll the dice, so to speak, in hopes that our problems do not get worse. In reality, you have two basic choices when you try to influence behavior: You can either wait for a problem to explode, or you can have a discussion about the problem before it explodes. If you believe in the decision you are influencing another person to make, then you need to get your hands a bit dirty now and then.

It's a stumbling block for all of us, but sometimes we have to ask questions that may cause pain. Instead of feeling bad about this immediate discomfort, you need to believe in something bigger.

IS IT MEAN, OR IS IT MERCIFUL?

There's no sugarcoating it: The most challenging part of influencing is asking the more difficult questions. These are the questions that are sometimes referred to as "pain" questions. In the end, success or failure often comes down to one thing: Can you create pain without creating conflict?

I received an email from a former client I deeply respect. She wrote that she had just asked some of those "pain" questions to a client, successfully. The process of forcing her client to look at the most difficult aspects of his resistance to change, however, made her "feel a little mean."

Those four words made me stop what I was doing, take a deep breath, and swallow hard. At that moment, I had to accept the fact that I had failed my client. I had failed to teach this person the most important lesson I could ever teach her. When you force someone to answer a difficult question—a question that makes another person feel the pain of not taking action, you are not being aggressive. You are, in fact, being empathetic.

I'll go a step further. I firmly believe it's one of the most sincere acts of kindness you can offer another human being. We've all seen people who are struggling at home or at work, and we want to help them. Anyone can come to the rescue with his or her wonderful ideas that dictate what the other person should do. It's a comfortable conversation, but it never creates change. It's the tougher road, but ultimately, the one that gets you to your destination.

It hurts to be asked where their children are when people are fighting with their spouse, but the answer can lead a couple to therapy. It hurts to be asked what impact not supporting a corporate directive could have on a new, starry-eyed manager, but the answer can save a career.

The process of influence isn't ruled simply by a tactic. It must be accompanied by an emotion. That emotion is one of empathy. You have to believe in the tough questions you ask, and then you will succeed. You'll succeed in the art of influence, and you'll succeed because you are exemplifying the art of caring about another person. When you ask difficult questions, it is never out of meanness. Think of it as compassionate and possibly life changing. Once confronted with the tragedy so many endure because of their inability to make tough decisions on their own, you see that these questions are, in fact, merciful.

If you can cross this bridge, and believe, then in the end you'll get to do what so many cannot: You'll *save* things. You get to save both people and businesses, because the path you took required discipline and courage. The results you initiated changed another person's life. You were the one who helped someone move past his or her fear of change, and into the future. Doing something like that is never mean. It's quite the contrary. It's merciful, and it is something to be profoundly proud of.

Never call another person's baby ugly!

Make no mistake about it: There is a fine line between "helpful" and "obnoxious." If you are not careful, you will find yourself telling the person you want to influence what his or her problem is. That would be the equivalent of calling someone's baby ugly! The steps in this process, and the questions that support it, are designed to let the person you are influencing define his or her own problem. Wouldn't leading someone to find his own solution through the use of your questions be a better alternative?

Think like a therapist

When's the last time you went to a therapist? Having never been to one myself (he says, nervously), my guess is that with a good therapist you probably experienced many of the concepts we discuss in this book being played out in your sessions.

Let's start with your first visit. A good therapist doesn't typically open up the conversation with a handshake, a smile, and a hearty, "What seems to be your problem today?" That question has to be earned. That's where the strategy of asking open questions, actively listening, aiming your questions, and avoiding problems come in. Adhering to this strategy establishes trust, and a good therapist will start right here, just like us.

Once trust is earned, a good therapist will gently begin to move toward the problem through his or her questions. There won't be a lot of guesswork here because while earning trust, he or she is gathering information, and trying to identify the challenges you are struggling with, just like us.

Most importantly, however, good therapists begin to distinguish themselves when they don't just successfully uncover the problem that has probably been told to many others before this visit. They distinguish themselves when they avoid the temptation to "fix it," and instead ask more questions, seeking to help both of you better understand the problem, just like us.

The funny thing is, I'm willing to bet most good therapists have a pretty good idea of your problem before you even get comfortable in your seat. I suppose they could go ahead and address it, and tell you what to do about it, but do you really think that's going to help you discover something you didn't already know, or provide any real chance of bringing about a significant change in behavior? Of course not!

We don't need to think of this process as some aggressive or mean-spirited conversation. We can think of it as a conversation we would have with someone we truly care about and want to help. We can think like a therapist. It's a shame that so frequently we don't.

Each and every question within these three steps, in its own way, serves to move an individual deeper into the problem. A great example of this point can be illustrated in a proverb called "For Want of a Nail." Various versions of the proverb have appeared through the years, from Richard III of England all the way back in 1485, to Ben Franklin in 1758, to right here and now. I have carried this proverb with me for over twenty years because this poem represents *exactly* what I am attempting to teach you.

FOR WANT OF A NAIL

> For want of a nail, the shoe was lost.
> For want of a shoe, the horse was lost.
> For want of a horse, the rider was lost.
> For want of a rider, the message was lost.
> For want of a message, the battle was lost.
> For want of a battle, the war was lost.
> For want of a war, the kingdom was lost.
> And all for the want of a nail.

People do not look at the impact of most of their problems. If they did, if *we* did, we would all make different decisions in our lives.

You *must* learn to get the people you are looking to influence to look down the road further and deeper at their problems. Using a sequence of questions referred to as *identifying, developing,* and *impact probes* does just that.

Enterprise and the Vinnie-Mobile

I've never been one for big cars; I just don't feel right in a big car. I'm a compact man. But when I flew into Albany one day, and bellied up to the counter for my Enterprise compact, a friendly fresh face who had other plans greeted me. His name was Vinnie, and as a twenty-five-year veteran sales trainer, I was looking forward to the conversation.

Vinnie looked up my reservation, smiled, and with my license and credit card in hand, we started the process of getting me behind the wheel of his small car. After all, I am a compact man.

There was some idle chitchat, and then a harmless question. "Where will you be taking the car, Mr. Jolles?" A harmless answer followed. "I'm heading to Keene Valley to conduct three days of sales training in the Adirondacks." I thought I saw Vinnie smile, but that might have been my imagination.

"Have you checked the weather report, Mr. Jolles?" Of course I had. (I not only have over two million miles of air travel under my belt over my career, I wrote a best-selling book on travel!) What self-respecting road warrior goes on a trip and doesn't check the weather report where he is traveling? I could sense where this conversation might be going and I wasn't having any of it.

"Yes, Vinnie, I've checked the weather. Why do you ask?" The small grin was gone, and a sincere look took its place. "Because there's always a chance the weather can change, and I think you might want to rent something a little bigger. I think you might want to rent a four-wheel-drive vehicle."

This kid was overmatched. I had looked at the weather report carefully, and seen that there was nothing more than rain predicted. I was curious, just the same, so we spoke about price. The vehicle was significantly more than the one I was planning to rent, but Vinnie seemed sincerely concerned. He offered to drop the price a little bit, but I still wasn't biting. Then Vinnie asked me a question that stopped me in my tracks. It was simple and yet brilliant. He calmly asked me, "What if the weather changes?"

I looked at him somewhat dumfounded, and he went on to say, "Well, I ask you that question because I was born and raised here in Albany. I know the Adirondacks well, and I know Keene Valley. The weather can be very volatile there and can change rather quickly. What if the weather changes on you, Mr. Jolles?"

I stammered a bit, and Vinnie bore in. "You will be driving well over 100 miles each way. What effect do you think this will have on your business trip, and the next location you might need to get to if you are driving a compact car?" Not only was I concerned about the safety of the compact I was considering, I had concerns about getting home to see my daughter performing in a play. It was a one-night performance, and I had never missed a performance. Getting back to Albany was critical. I told Vinnie I'd take the bigger four-wheel-drive vehicle, moved past the price issue, and headed to the mountains.

Well, the weather did change and it snowed, for three days. The snow total was between 16 and 20 inches. My big four-wheel-drive Ford seemed almost to laugh at the snow. I felt safe in what I was now calling the "Vinnie-Mobile," and the trip was a success. I made it out of the Adirondacks, and I had no trouble getting back to Albany to catch my flight.

By asking me that simple question, a question I conveniently avoided asking myself, an Enterprise employee saved me from missing a life event with my youngest child. While he was at it, he helped me avoid other costs a delay would have incurred, and ultimately saved me money. The Vinnie-Mobile may have been a few dollars more a day to rent, but it became the best bargain on the road to drive. Vinnie also earned a client for life, my respect, and my appreciation.

The "Vinnie-Mobile" dug out and ready to go!

* * *

FOR WANT OF AN UPGRADE

For want of an upgrade, the flight was lost.
For want of a flight, the play was lost.
For want of a play, the moment was lost.
For want of a moment, the memory was lost.
For want of a memory, the bond was lost.
For want of a bond, the relationship was lost.
And all for the want of an upgrade.

THE CASE OF THE FINANCIAL HOBBY

Impact Probes

The Need: You want to finish this sequence of probes off with one, final question that allows the person you are influencing to reflect on the problem as a whole.

The Tactic: With the problem *identified* and *developed*, you have one final question: an *impact probe*.

Identifying: "What challenges have you experienced with some of the more aggressive moves you've made in the market?"

Developing: "How much have you lost up to this point?"

"What had you intended to use that money for?"

"And?"

The Example: "What would be the consequences of experiencing multiple losses like this on your portfolio as a whole?"

So there you are. You have your teeth into a problem, and like a Doberman, you won't let go. I have seen others who have been so excited with the progress of their questioning that they had trouble containing themselves and started smiling.

You are experiencing strong emotions. Now is not the time to show your joy with the newfound skills you have acquired! Watch your body language, your tone, and, for goodness' sake, your facial expressions. The probing sequence can be traumatic, and your ability to mirror the expressions of those you are communicating with sincerely will serve you well.

Those who manipulate *inadvertently display a sense of satisfaction when hearing of another person's pain. It represents a personal triumph.*

Those who influence *display empathy when hearing of another person's pain. It represents trust, and they too feel that pain.*

A POSITIVE PERSPECTIVE

Until now, I have not presented the most positive slant to this most difficult task within the art of influence. In the past when I encountered someone who felt my suggestions were too negative or aggressive, I passed it off as someone who simply missed the point of my message. People are motivated by the consequences of their actions. That's a fact—not a feeling.

When changing a person's behavior, consequence is more powerful than value.

I have also had some healthy debates regarding the possibility of showing value through my questions as opposed to consequence. I resisted. "Is a cigarette smoker unaware that he will feel healthier if he stops smoking?" "Is a struggling employee unaware that his quality of life will improve if he works harder to get along with others on his team?"

Consequence Is a Very Powerful Motivator

My dad was a smoker for many, many years. As he told me one day, "When I joined the navy at sixteen (he and his father lied about his age), I wasn't a smoker for about an hour. When the first cigarette break was announced I continued to swab the deck. An hour later I grabbed a cigarette like everyone else."

Thirty years later we were begging my dad to give up his two-pack-a-day habit. We tried everything possible, meaning we tried every solution possible. He just couldn't stop.

My father was one of seven brothers. When his first brother was diagnosed with terminal cancer, he was angry. When his second brother was diagnosed with terminal cancer, he took his cigarettes and threw them in a bush and never smoked again. Consequence is a very powerful motivator.

* * *

That's my story, and I'm sticking with it! Think back on most of the decisions you have made recently. Did you buy that last car because you had an irresistible urge for that new car smell, or was it because you just finished picking up the old car from the shop—for the third time in three months—and gasped when you saw the bill? Did you change jobs because you just had to experience the joys of meeting new people, or was it because you were fed up trying to reason things out with your existing boss? I rest my case . . . sort of.

Can it be argued that some people are motivated by positive consequences as opposed to negative consequence?

It took me about a decade to admit it, but the answer is yes. There are those who are motivated by value. I want to go on record to tell you that many more of our decisions are based on consequence than on value, but I can no longer ignore the fact that there are those who base certain decisions strictly on value.

For instance, if you ask someone who retires and moves to Florida why he made that decision, he may tell you, "If I had to go through one more lousy winter up North I'd go crazy!" Sounds like a decision based on consequence. However, others may say, "I came down to Florida some years ago to play golf, and I had such a great time I decided someday I'd move here!" Sounds like a decision based on value.

Fortunately, from a process angle, little changes in the way you work with someone who is motivated by value. The same three question types apply with one, slight, *positive* change. Instead of asking about the negative effects that can be expected, the questions move to the positive effects that can be expected. In other words, rather than asking someone, "What other concerns do you have about not solving this?" you might ask, "What other benefits do you think you'll gain by solving this?"

Please remember, the decision you make to influence based on consequence or value is *not* yours. It is irrelevant if this is the way *you* would like to be influenced. What is relevant is the way the person you are looking to influence is affected by your questions.

Well, that's it. What you have read is crucial when engaging in the art of influence. A lifetime of working with this process permits me to say that the steps contained within this stage are far more difficult to implement than you might think. That's just fine! The final chapter of this book outlines the actual implementation of this process, so fear not. With hard work and repetition, the process will become muscle memory before you know it.

5

Committing to Change

Those who manipulate *believe the more you ask for a commitment, the greater your chances of success.*

Those who influence *believe you earn the right to ask for someone's commitment.*

So here we are—after methodically creating trust, we earned the right to enter into a conversation—to a guarded area many don't allow us to enter. Once allowed in, we not only asked questions so as to identify this problem, we carefully, and empathetically, dug deeper. As a result, we allowed those who were feeling this pain to understand the true ramifications of their actions, and thus we created urgency. Take a deep breath, because you're on the cusp of applying influence and changing another person's mind. Did you miss it? Take a look at the definition that appears in the first chapter of this book.

At its core, when you are applying influence and changing another person's mind, you are taking an idea, planting that idea in the other person's brain, and making the person feel as if he or she thought of it.

People don't just show up ready to put a patch on their arm to stop a cigarette habit that has consumed them for a lifetime. Let me take a moment and connect the dots for you.

- In the *decision cycle* you learned that the problem shapes the need. A cigarette smoker doesn't wake up, yawn, and announce he's kicking the habit. When someone experiences a problem keeping up with his children on the playground, or with his friends in a pick-up basketball game, he starts asking about suggestions to kick the habit.

- When you learned about the key elements of trust, among other things, you learned to *aim* your questions and begin with the end in mind. That means entering into conversations about problems we *know* we can solve. In the smoker's case, it means asking about the physical activity that he is currently engaged in.

- When you learned the *blueprint for changing minds*, you learned how to take these issues that may appear to be mildly annoying to another person, and to go deeper. That means asking *developing probes* that track the problem further, and *impact probes* that allow those we are attempting to influence see the ultimate consequences of their actions. You learned to create urgency.

At this point in the conversation, needs are beginning to appear in the other person's mind, and you have been anything but a passive observer in this process! You have been instrumental in influencing the need that is appearing in that other person's mind. What's more, because we have these conversations around issues we know can influence, these developing needs have occurred naturally around the particular strengths we've been aiming at all along. The other person is about to cross a critical decision point: a decision for change.

Is what I've just described influence, or manipulation? Once again, let's use intent as our filter. We can wait for a spot on our loved one's lung to appear, or we can have a conversation about it. I ask again, is what I've just described influence, or manipulation? I proudly and without hesitation stand on the side of influence.

This one decision point is a critical hurtle for us all, and one that many struggle with for a lifetime. Well, like watching the dawn of a new day, change is just about to occur.

The most important question that's never asked

When it comes to asking for committing questions, we've heard them all:

- "What's it going to take to get you into this car today?"
- "Is Tuesday good, or is Wednesday better?"
- "Other than price, what would keep you from buying this toaster today?"
- "If I could prove that our vacuum cleaner is better than any other on the market, would you buy one today?"

They're all interesting questions, and each may actually have its own place in a particular conversation, but there's one question that no one asks. Ironically, if you are trying to commit someone to the change she is contemplating, there could not be a more important question. The question is simply this: "Are you committed to making a change?"

There are a few other ways to ask this question including, "Is now a good time to look at some alternatives?" "Do you think it's worthwhile looking at some alternatives?" and "Do you want to fix this or not?" If you want to take the temperature in a particular conversation, this question will let you know exactly where you stand.

Don't think for a moment this question is coming from left field. Tracking that *decision cycle* once again provides the logic behind this question. Remember, coming out of the *acknowledge stage,* the first decision someone goes through, like crossing a line in the sand, is, "Do I want to make a change or not?" If you've worked your way through trust and urgency, you've moved with the person to this part of the cycle and earned the right to ask that question for him. "Are you ready to do something about this issue?"

If the answer you receive is no (quite frankly that answer is rather rare when you've taken the time and the trouble to ask the more difficult questions that create urgency), we'll stop right there. It would be a waste of time to offer a solution to a problem someone has just admitted he still doesn't want to fix. We're not giving up yet because we can still tackle this as an objection later in this book. However, if the answer to the question is yes, congratulations, you've just changed someone's mind, and psychologically committed him to that change. Something tells me we'll have a solution that will address the needs that are now appearing.

We've finally arrived at the solution. How exciting! Strangely enough, I have little interest in the solution. Imagine that; we've finally arrived at a solution, and it's almost irrelevant to me. Anyone can offer solutions. When you learn *how to change minds,* you learn that the struggle lies in trying to get another person to commit to solving the problem you want to solve. Ironically, when I conduct two-day workshops, I spend only about fifteen minutes on the actual solution. I spend the rest of the sixteen hours working on teaching the various tactics of influence, on getting people to commit to change, and on what to do after people have made that commitment. However, when you do discuss a solution, there are two pretty important words I'd like you to remember. Then we'll go for the real close.

Two Taped Words

When I worked for Xerox as a sales trainer, like all the other sales trainers, I watched a lot of role-plays. Most classes I taught were two weeks long, and consisted of six students for every trainer. Every morning began with a filmed role-play that was followed by a coaching session with the trainer. There was a lot of pressure on these role-plays, so, to compensate for this, Xerox created small role-play rooms containing a desk, two chairs, and a camera. This allowed each role-play to be performed in relative privacy (that is, not counting the monitor in the classroom where the rest of the class sat and watched the role-play, but I digress).

I experimented with all sorts of things I could post in that role-play room to help students. I tried tacking up key words, inspirational sayings, and even a picture or two of beach scenes designed to be calming in nature. Then I finally arrived at two words that did the trick. I taped these two words to the desk so the person selling could see them throughout the role-play. The words were "you said."

* * *

Those words were my reminder that we ask questions, listen, and let those we are communicating with paint their own picture. We work meticulously to allow the people we are communicating with to own the conversation we are having. It's not about us; it's about them. If we do this, when we get to the solution, we get to use the words "you said."

The solutions we bring to the table are not coming from left field, and just in case the person sitting across from us needs a reminder, there's nothing like saying, "Another reason I'm making this recommendation is that *you said* you were looking for a simple way to accomplish this goal. Let me tell you exactly how simple this is."

The words "you said" have an amazing way of putting someone right back into the conversation. These words act as a reminder that the solution isn't for you; it's for her. Think for a moment the last time someone was talking to you and you heard the words "you said" inserted into the conversation. Assuming you *did* say it, that person sure got your attention!

At this point we've done an amazing job gaining a commitment to change, and offering a solution that addresses someone's specific needs, but it's not time to celebrate just yet. I've spent thirty years of my life watching this story unfold, and guess what can often happen next? Nothing. And the reason nothing often happens is that, although we've gained a commitment to change, and shown a logical solution, we never really close the deal. Well, let's fix that right now!

The whole concept of asking for a true commitment from another brings with it many misunderstandings. The confusion runs deeps within industries that have dedicated personnel obsessed with selling and gaining commitment. I believe many, including me early on in my own career, are sometimes a little reluctant to challenge the old conventional methods of gaining commitment. So let's start by offering a few facts and some rather strong opinions that should do away with some of these ridiculous old myths.

Myth 1. The more you ask someone to commit to a change, the greater your chances of success.

Interesting statement. So much has been written about the theory "more is better," when it comes to gaining a commitment. It's been said by many that the more you do this, the greater your chance of gaining that commitment. Sales teams for decades have preached "Always be closing" as a kind symbolic mantra. I have one small issue with this theory: It could not be further from the truth.

I suppose there was a time, when orange leisure suits roamed the earth, that this approach to gaining commitment might have worked. But if by chance it ever worked back then, it sure doesn't work now. In fact, I believe constantly asking someone for a commitment can backfire.

One of my favorite studies, conducted by Xerox, took dead aim at this particular myth. The study found that when someone was asked for a commitment, and that request was followed by the answer "no," the chances of gaining a commitment fell by 24 percent. Personally, I'm surprised it wasn't even higher.

Why, you ask? A lot of it has to do with ego. No one wants to feel manipulated. A "no" is usually a "no," particularly when there is an emotional issue on the table. In fact, I believe once we say no, there is a quiet chant running through our heads saying, "I said no, and I meant no, and I'm not letting some fast-talking, manipulative person change my mind!"

I just can't get behind the notion that continuing to pound away by asking someone to commit to something, and believing the more you do this, the better your chances become, can ever really work. All you are doing, in this case, is forcing the person you are hoping to influence to dig his heels in even deeper.

Watch a good negotiator, and you'll see more proof of a methodical approach to avoid backing anyone into a corner. Asking someone to commit over and over again simply hardens the position of the person whose mind you are trying to change. A lot of care needs to be taken when asking for a commitment, and it begins with being well aware of the fact that you won't have multiple opportunities.

Myth 2. There are a thousand effective ways to gain a commitment, and each is good in its own way.

Why is it that so many of us believe that more is somehow better? There sure are a lot of books on the subject of gaining commitment, and most boast of the vast number of ways to do this. Again, many believe that there is somehow strength in numbers. I say that this is a myth and nothing more.

I have not only seen, but have been recruited many times to deliver, programs that teach only the skills involved in gaining commitment. The money is good, and the misguided audiences seem to show up. The problem for me is the ethics involved in teaching these ridiculous programs.

I mention ethics because the mere fact of obsessing on this final part of the process of influence demonstrates a lack of any persuasive skills whatsoever. *You earn the right to ask a person to commit to change.* Why in the world would you want to spend an entire day learning the "tricks" of how to ask someone to change? I would rather spend an entire day learning a process and path to *earn* the right to ask someone that question.

The Trainer Who Went to the Dark Side

Back in the mid-1980s, while working with Xerox, one of my jobs was to supervise and teach every new sales trainer the company hired. We had a reputation for some of the finest sales training and trainers in the industry, and I was fiercely proud of my contribution.

We achieved our reputation because we broke every part of the selling process down to a series of tactics. These tactics would ultimately lead a seller to an actual close. In a typical two-week program, we spent about nine days teaching a student how to get to the close, and about ten minutes on the actual close.

Everything was first rate, even the facility where we taught. Xerox Document University (XDU) and its 2.4 million square feet of office space, sat on 2,400 acres, housed more than 1,000 students, and was state-of-the-art from top to bottom. We were considered the "Green Berets" of sales trainers and that reputation was both a blessing and a curse. Hiring companies and headhunters were always lurking, trying to lure one of our sales trainers away from our company.

During my time as supervisor, I lost only one sales trainer to another company. This sales trainer left Xerox to teach one-day closing seminars across the country. His loss was a double blow to me, and I took it personally. It was bad enough to lose a high-level performer in whom we had invested a lot of time and energy, but losing him to teach closing seminars? I would have preferred he go sell for another company, or manage for another company, but teaching one-day closing seminars? It went against everything I was taught to believe in.

I took the loss of this person personally. You earn the right to ask someone to commit to a change. When you use the skills that are necessary to influence change, there are many steps involved. Asking for a commitment is the easy part; earning the right to ask for that commitment is the hard part. That's where the work, study, and elbow grease come in. We at Xerox laughed at these other programs and looked down our noses at those who taught them. Now, under my watch, we were losing one of our own; it bothered me then, and it bothers me to this day.

I don't know whatever happened to that Xerox sales trainer, and I honestly don't even remember his name because from that day on I have simply referred to this person as the "trainer who went to the dark side." My guess is that after the closing seminars dried up, he spent some time teaching one more one-day program on objection-handling skills. When all you do is hammer people with closing tactics, you better be well versed in objection-handling skills!

* * *

Look closely at this snake oil that is being peddled, and what you will really find are a couple of legitimate tactics sandwiched within a number of approaches that look more like con games than commitments.

There is no need to obsess on this stage of the process, and there are not a thousand ways to gain commitment. There are more like four, and I'll show you one that should make this final step to influence a whole lot easier.

Myth 3. You don't really need to ask for a commitment to gain a commitment.

Hmm. Just imagine. . . .

Yes, ladies and gentlemen, because you've learned the lesson taught in this book, you will no longer have to ask someone to commit to anything! Now that you've learned how to change minds, on their own, and with no prompting from you, people will commit in droves to whatever you wish!

Asking a person for his or her commitment is not only a natural part of the persuasive process, it's a necessary part of the process. It is ludicrous to risk all the work you have put into influence in the search for vague "persuasive signals." No, there's one true way to find out if another person is committed to change, and that's to ask.

Myth 4. There's only one thing worth gaining a commitment to, and that's a commitment to change.

If I agreed to that one, I would shoot down any credibility I might have established. It is just not true. When seeking a commitment, the goal is to search for the highest realistic level of commitment.

This is not to suggest that this highest realistic level of commitment might not be a little more creative than you are accustomed to. It seems that often the commitments we seek are just not as black and white as we would hope for. This book outlines numerous scenarios that require the skills of influence to help you change minds. You can help a loved one realize that smoking is unhealthy, change a friend's outlook on his risk-taking behavior, help a client see the long-term effects of treating her financial planning as a hobby, improve a child's homework habits—the list goes on.

Even when adhering to all the tactics you've learned about when influencing behavior, flexibility can be one of your strongest weapons. Sometimes the commitment you may be seeking will be achieved by taking smaller steps. The goal is to achieve the highest, most realistic level of commitment.

THE SUMMARY COMMITMENT

Now put the myths behind you and prepare yourself for a simple, four-step approach to asking for a commitment. I have chosen this approach because, as you will see, it is a natural fit to finish off the process you have learned, and there is a lot of room for personalization.

⬥THE CASE OF THE HOMEWORK HASSLE

The Summary Commitment

Background: Homework time has never been the most pleasant time in your house, but lately it has become a huge source of stress for you and your child. Intimidation didn't work, and neither did punishment. As a matter of fact, it created even greater tension in the family, and an even greater disdain for homework as a whole. Fortunately, you've committed to learning how to change minds, and after following the processes we've outlined, you have successfully led your child to buy into a solution, and there are hugs all around.

The Tactic: Now comes perhaps the most important step of all, and that's not only gaining a commitment to change, but making sure that the commitments are kept. You're so close to change you can practically taste it!

Step 1: Confirm benefits

The first step of the *summary commitment* involves one last check with the person you are trying to persuade. Most people do not understand just how powerful this last check can be. Let me show you what I mean. Read the next statement, stop, and without reading any further, try to anticipate what the next step of this process would be.

Don't you agree that by doing your homework, you are going to see the results you said you were looking for?

Okay, now what do you think my next question will be if the answer received is yes. I believe most people will assume a question requiring a commitment is sure to follow, and, in my humble opinion, that's the genius of this first step. No one would dare answer yes to that question if he did not intend to go ahead with a solution.

Uh, yes it does everything I want it to do, but, uh, no, I don't want to change.

That, my friends, happens to be the biggest strength of the summary commitment. In a sense, confirming benefits provides a trial close to your conversation. If there is an objection, the person you are seeking a commitment from will push back right here. It does not make me happy to hear a "no" at this point of the conversation, but so be it. At least you won't be battling an ego as well as the objection. Remember, you have not asked for a commitment, nor have you backed anyone into a corner. You merely asked if the solution talked about was an appropriate one. If it wasn't, we'll clarify the issue, move to our objection tactics, and give it our best shot.

If the answer is yes, then we'll smile. Why would you hesitate now? There are never guarantees, but I would feel pretty confident at this point and would consider the chances of gaining a solid commitment extremely high.

THE CASE OF THE HOMEWORK HASSLE

Confirm Benefits

The Need: You have created trust, urgency, and put forth a solution that lines up with the problems you are helping your child solve.

The Tactic: You want to transition and gain a true commitment from your child.

The Examples: "Don't you agree that by doing your homework, you are going to see the results you said you were looking for?"

~Or~

"Wouldn't you agree the solution we've come up with will not only improve your grades, but will make things a lot easier for you down the road?"

✳ ✳ ✳

What most people do not realize about *confirming benefits* is that by asking this first question, you are actually taking the temperature of the situation. That summary packs quite a psychological punch!

Step 2: Ask for a commitment

Well, what do you know? At last, it's time to ask for the final commitment. It's amazing how easy gaining a commitment really is when you've earned your right to ask the question. As I mentioned before, your strategy here should be to aim for the highest *realistic* level of commitment.

But how do you ask for a commitment? What words do you use? My recommendation would be to do it as simply as possible. This is a natural step, and the person you are influencing expects you to ask, so do it!

I'm always surprised when I work with people who persuade for a living; it seems that few of them have a favorite way of asking this question. I'm not a person who is very fond of canned or scripted responses, but I would recommend that you not search for your words here. There's a lot on the line, and you don't want your words, tone, or even facial expressions to betray you.

THINK IT OUT

Salespeople are a curious lot. Sit down with a few hearty souls who have made a living in this profession, and you'll pick up on all sorts of idiosyncrasies. Many will have a favorite place to meet clients, a favorite time of day to call clients, and even a favorite pen to use when they are trying to ink a deal and gain a commitment. With all these favorite moves and quirks, I'm always surprised, when I ask if they have a favorite way to ask a person for a commitment, that the answer is no.

It surprises me because there's a lot on the line here, and I have no idea why anyone would want to be searching for words here. Imagine how you would feel if you were on the doorstep of making a decision for change, struggling with the fear that goes along with it, and you heard this: "Don't you agree that by doing your homework, you are going to see the results you said you were looking for?" So far, so good, and let's assume the answer was yes. It's the next question that concerns me.

"Great, then I'd like, I mean do you think, well, uh, what I'm trying to say is, uh, will you do it?" Imagine being on the receiving end of that mess! Even if you had been on the verge of committing to making a change of some sort, I'm pretty sure you'd be backing out now.

There is a lot at stake here, and you've worked too hard to present an unsure side of yourself to the person you are influencing. If you're unsure of the solution you are asking someone to commit to, you can be sure she will be, too.

Remember, the summary commitment merely provides a structure that you can use with your favorite technique. There are many techniques used in asking customers for commitment in the business world; these same techniques can easily be applied to situations you face every day. Realistically, there are about a dozen legitimate approaches possible. Below are my four favorites.

◆THE CASE OF THE HOMEWORK HASSLE

Ask for a Commitment

The Need: You have confirmed that the solution you've proposed does in fact address your child's needs.

The Tactic: You want to seek the highest, realistic level of commitment you can from the person you are communicating with.

The Examples:

Assumptive: "When would you like to get started?"

If/then: "If we start with _____, then we can move to _____."

Alternate: "Would you like to start with just math, or would you prefer we approach your other classes this way too?"

Direct: "I'd love for you to get started with this today."

Once you understand what your highest realistic level of commitment is, you'll be in a better position to tailor your approach and the words you choose around that commitment.

Step 3: Discuss logistics

With a commitment in hand, you must stay focused and finish strong. The only thing left is to work out the logistics to implement the commitment that has been made. I have seen months of strategy go down the drain for lack of a proper follow-up after a verbal commitment was obtained.

Having conducted seminars for over thirty years, sometimes I feel like I've heard just about every question when it comes to teaching audiences how to change minds. Want to know one of the most frequently asked questions? "What's the most forgotten step of the process?" That's an easy one; it's forgetting to go over what happens after someone agrees to a change. The repercussions are serious because without this conversation, guess what often happens *after* someone agrees to change? We have good intentions to change, but buyer's remorse kicks in, a touch of fear of change joins the mix, and *nothing* happens.

There is a sense of euphoria that sweeps into the conversation when change is promised, and the actual logistics are often left behind. These logistics should not consist of your dictating the next moves, but rather a give-and-take regarding the next moves to be made. It's critical that you remain focused and continue along the path of influence.

THE CASE OF THE HOMEWORK HASSLE

Discuss Logistics

The Need: You want to build a path from agreement to action without getting lost in the excitement of an agreement.

The Tactic: A careful conversation regarding what happens next.

The Example: "That's great! So where do we go from here?"

~Or~

"Fantastic. I'll help set up the study environment you discussed, and I'll make sure everything is in place from this end. Then how about we sit down a week from today, double back, and see how things are going?"

If this doesn't persuade you, perhaps I should remind you of what comes next in the *decision cycle* of those you are influencing; it's the dreaded buyer's remorse! The smoother and better thought out you are here, the greater chance you have not just to change someone's mind, but to maintain the commitment you've earned.

Step 4: Reassure

Gaining a commitment from someone who is truly looking to make a change can be emotional. I have to admit that, although I felt it was a good idea to reassure the people I wanted to influence, I didn't add the *reassure* step to the process until years after I began teaching my methods. I'm not sure if it was that I just assumed most people did it, or that I had a blind spot. However, I've seen so many shaky decisions get reversed over the years by people who talked themselves out of commitments that I won't leave it out again.

The Most Forgotten Step in Closing

After teaching sales to many clients over decades of delivery, I think one of my favorite seminars was the hostage negotiation seminar I conducted in Baltimore twenty-two years ago. It was an exhilarating experience as I connected the world of selling to the world of hostage negotiation. My audience was receptive and engaged, but the presentation turned on a dime when I approached the concept of comforting those we are gaining commitments from.

I casually mentioned reassurance, and that I liked to reassure the person I've gained a commitment from. I never before placed that step in my materials, nor had I ever really pushed that hard for others to do this. I could hear my New York Life manager telling me, "Jolles, once you've made the sale, get out of the house!" The thinking was, if you had a commitment, any further conversation could only lead to disrupting the agreement you had already achieved. In the situation with the hostage negotiators, however, I felt that the risk of a buyer's remorse was worth the risk of throwing in a few comforting and reassuring words.

I guess you could say this was a hunch of mine, and the response was clear with one, dramatic story from a participant in the audience. Once I finished throwing out this final idea, a participant walked up to the microphone and began to speak.

Mr. Jolles, I happen to agree with your suggestion. Two months ago, I was on the phone communicating with an individual for almost forty hours. After twenty hours, I got the children out of the house. It took me ten more hours, and I got the wife out of the house. Ten hours later, I was able to reach an agreement to get the suspect out of the house. His last words to me were this: "I'm coming out, but not without my gun." It was the best I could do, and my last words to him were "Just go slow."

The suspect stepped out of the house onto the porch. I moved up the driveway slowly with the SWAT team by my side. The suspect looked out, he looked back, he looked out, he looked back. Then he blew his head off.

I had spent forty hours on the phone with this person and I can tell you that this was not the kind of person who intended to come out and put on a show. In an instant, he changed his mind. I will always wonder if I could have handled this differently. If the last words out of my mouth had been, "You are doing the right thing. I will be here every step of the way and everything I promised you will happen, I can assure you," I wonder if I could have saved his life.

Needless to say, this was an emotional moment for everyone at the seminar. I swallowed hard, finished the seminar, and since that day I have never again referred to this step as optional in the closing process.

* * *

The message is clear: People who have changed their minds will reconsider and wonder about the decisions they've made, particularly when these decisions required significant change. People fear change. Rather than hope they don't reconsider, give them something to think about when they do. Not if, but when, they reconsider, let them hear your voice in their minds telling them they made the right decision.

THE CASE OF THE HOMEWORK HASSLE

Reassure

The Need: You want to cement the commitment made with a careful statement that reassures your child.

The Tactic: A well-worded conclusion is needed.

The Example: "The hard part is behind us. Now comes the easy part, which is getting you up and on your way. I'll be here every step of the way to help you in any way I can. I'm so glad we were able to have this talk."

With the summary commitment now broken down for you into four manageable steps, I hope this portion of persuasion no longer gives you unnecessary anxiety. Here are four additional things to watch out for so you can add polish to what I hope will be a stellar finish to your conversations.

1. **Watch your tone**. By tone, I am referring not just to "what" you are saying, but to "how" you are saying it. Up to now, I have only discussed the words involved in gaining a commitment. There are a lot of emotions involved in changing someone's behavior, so the way you say things goes a long way to making this an easier process.

2. **Watch your face.** You have lined up your words, and your tone supports your words, but you must be on top of your facial expressions. They can be your best friend or your worst enemy. My suggestion is, be in the moment. If you are feeling understanding, be understanding. If you look unsure, those you are conversing with will feel unsure. If you look confident, others will feel confident.

3. **Watch your finish.** Another pitfall to avoid involves how you finish your conversation. When you ask someone for commitment, make sure your words are short and to the point. Remember, you have just finished a rather lengthy conversation. Therefore, there is certainly no need to go over a list of long-winded explanations once again. You've made your case, you've gained your commitment; don't linger!

4. **Watch your transition.** You might be surprised by what gives most people difficulty in asking someone for a commitment. Over and over again, it's the transition to the commitment that trips people up.

In a sense, we flounder about, hoping a moment will just magically present itself, the sea will part, and the moment will be there for us! I say, let's stop waiting, and let's create our own moment instead. My suggestion is to move into that commitment with three simple words: "Don't you agree?"

There is no real secret to gaining a commitment, nor need for you to obsess about it. Earning the right to ask someone for a commitment by logically walking in someone else's shoes and following that person's decision cycle should provide you with all the confidence you need. Now all we have to do is figure out how to get this conversation started.

6

Initiating Change

Those who manipulate *see an opening as a way to mislead someone into engaging in a conversation.*

Those who influence *see an opening as a way to determine if there are mutual benefits in engaging in a conversation.*

As the shampoo commercial states, "You only have one chance to make a first impression." When preparing for a critical conversation that involves the influence of another person's opinion or behavior, that "one chance" usually boils down to about forty-five seconds. These are precious seconds and should be handled as carefully as possible.

When I think of an opening, I think of it as a topic sentence. A topic sentence is intended to serve as an overview of the paper you are writing. Your opening should act like an overview of the conversation you are about to have.

The opening tactics I will be showing you are flexible and can be applied to the opening of any conversation, regardless of your relationship with those with whom you are communicating. The verbiage will change, but the process will not. Personally, I think the most difficult conversation to initiate is one with someone who doesn't know you very well, so, to make my point, this chapter will focus there.

Be warned: It is not easy to initiate a frank conversation that will ultimately require the change of behavior in another individual. There is no "magic pill" here, but rather a set of actions, which, if adhered to carefully, should maximize your chances of having a conversation. This, in turn, will allow you the best opportunity to influence another.

Let's face it. If you can't get past the opening, you won't have much use for everything we've covered thus far. Let me show you the simplest approach I know to get people to allow you to peer into their lives.

THE CASE OF THE RELATIONSHIP RUT

Initiating Change

Background: You've been married for ten years. There was a time when you used to talk, but the first child came, and then the second. After that there were a couple of promotions, two cars, and a mortgage. Now, a decade later, you and your spouse seem to be sharing separate lives.

The Tactic: You want to open up a conversation, but you want to proceed cautiously. This has never been an easy conversation between the two of you.

Step 1: The introduction

This first step is rather basic. It is not exactly rocket science to tell a person who you are and what organization you represent. This is obviously not necessary in a close relationship or with someone we know well, but with those we do not know well, this step can be a little tricky.

How much do you want the other person to know? Perhaps you are the largest dealership in the area. You could make this a part of your introduction. Perhaps you are experienced in the topic you are about to discuss. This would certainly contribute to your credibility. My suggestion is to tread lightly, providing just enough information to create credibility, but not too much information so as to overwhelm the other person. Remember this important rule:

The most powerful benefits are the ones people discover on their own.

The key is this: It is more advantageous for you not to tip your hand as to your solution within your opening. In some situations, this cannot be helped, but even in a worst-case scenario, take it easy with going into detail about how wonderful your solution or your company is. The art of influence involves drawing others to your solution, and making that solution their own. For the sake of this case study between a married couple, no example is necessary. However, if you are applying the principles of this book to those who do not know you, a simple who you are, and where you are from should do fine.

Step 2: The hook

Remember, if someone can't wait to have a conversation with you, the opening will not be as critical as I seem to be making it, but if you are trying to initiate a conversation involving a sensitive subject, or a conversation with

someone who barely knows you, this is the most important step you will learn in the opening. At its deepest level,
the *hook* provides an answer to a critical question that
most of us have on our minds. It provides a WIFM, which
stands for "what's in it for me?" This little acronym, in my
opinion, requires a great deal of skill and attention.

To better explain the hook, let me offer a quick lesson
in human psychology. The simple truth is that most people
in this world are motivated by greed. Now this statement
comes from yours truly, one of the most optimistic people
you will ever meet.

Ask yourself why you bought this book. Did you feel
sorry for the book? I'm assuming you bought this book
because you felt you could learn some ideas relating to
the act of changing another person's mind by using influence instead of manipulation. I think you did that because
you believed this would help you become more successful. Your definition of success may have little to do with
money, but may, in fact, relate to happiness, personal satisfaction, or simply bettering yourself. I don't want to burst
your bubble, but I would call that greed.

Is greed a bad thing? Actually, it is just the opposite.
You see, once you understand that most people desire to be
more successful, you also begin to realize how much easier
they are to influence. Consider these two different scenarios
relating to a person whose mind you want to change.

SCENARIO ONE

This first person could care less about his own personal success or failure. What's more, he's not particularly concerned

with his own health or his family responsibilities. What exactly would be in it for him, to consider change? You might find him easy to meet, but to initiate change, let alone change his mind, might be extremely difficult. There's nothing in it for him even to consider change.

SCENARIO TWO

This second person is much different. This person has a driven desire for success. Her family is precious to her as is her relationship with her husband. Furthermore, she is well aware that her personal health is vital to protect all that she loves. She may not be the easiest person to meet with, but if you can connect what you want to talk about to what's in it for her, your chances are good that she'll sit down and talk with you.

Which person would you rather meet when attempting to initiate change? Greed really isn't a bad thing at all, now, is it?

THE CASE OF THE RELATIONSHIP RUT

The Hook

The Need: You want to get your spouse to sit down and calmly discuss your relationship; not typically an easy topic for your spouse.

The Tactic: You want to use the *hook* to get him to sit down and have a sincere and open conversation regarding your relationship.

The Examples: "Pat, I really want to sit down and talk about something that's not just important to me, but that will make our relationship stronger as well."

The challenge of writing an effective hook is to provide just enough information without giving away too much information. Enticing someone with a well-worded hook sometimes requires a rather creative balancing act.

It is really not a question of good or bad luck for most people who successfully initiate a conversation. It is often a question of appealing to someone's desire to be more successful. Try to figure out what would be an effective hook for the person you are looking to persuade, and see if this doesn't contribute mightily to getting that conversation started.

Step 3: The process

Imagine, if you will, that you are about to be approached by someone who you suspect is going to try to convince you to do something you don't really want to do. Your stomach starts to churn as you prepare for what is sure to be a lecture. Oh boy, you know just how this conversation is going to go.

When we are put into a position that requires the influence of another, we are guilty until proven innocent. If the last conversation you had was with someone who had no interest in listening to you, or asked you no questions, or dumped a solution on the table with a dozen boring reasons as to why it would benefit you, it would only be natural for you to assume the worst.

Therefore, if the the hook is the most critical step of the opening tactic, the *process* is certainly a strong second.

People need to know up front, in the first forty-five seconds, *how* you intend to proceed, and that is the exact intent of the the process for your opening.

Telling someone up front that you intend to listen to her and ask questions sets a completely different tone from what most people are accustomed to. Why would you want to keep this a secret? Here is an example of the *process* step within an initial conversation.

THE CASE OF THE RELATIONSHIP RUT

The Process

The Need: You don't want to sit and beg your spouse to make changes in your relationship. You want to use questions that will allow him to arrive at this decision, and own it.

The Tactic: Because you frequently dictated the changes you wanted your spouse to make in previous conversations, these talks did not go well. This time you want him to understand not just *what* you want to talk about, but *how* you would like to talk about it.

The Examples: "I don't want to tell you what to do, Pat. I simply want to talk about it, and that means I need to ask questions and listen."

You are in control of the *process*. If you intend to take notes, and if you want to demonstrate visually that you intend to listen to someone, all you need to do is ask.

Guilty until proven innocent? Fine. Clear the air up front and let others know exactly how you intend to proceed. This will eliminate many unspoken objections and prepare all involved for an intelligent and productive conversation.

Step 4: The time

This final step is intended to provide an exact sense of how long the conversation will take. It is simple and fast but controversial. Allow me to present two views to you.

One argument is to eliminate this step completely. Why lock yourself into a specific time constraint when you could potentially be shortening your own conversation? It is a simple question that raises a very good point. Often you will be eliminating your own chances for a longer, more comprehensive conversation. Argument made and understood.

The other side of the argument is even more basic, however. If you were to eliminate time, you would be forced to say things like, "Can I have a few minutes of your time?" Remember, the *process* step that preceded this step makes the point that we are guilty until proven innocent. With this in mind, you must ask yourself, What does "a few minutes" really mean from someone who is going to try to change your mind? "I need a few minutes" is often answered with a roll of the eyes and a quick excuse as to why this isn't a good time to talk.

THE CASE OF THE RELATIONSHIP RUT

The Time

The Need: You are trying to demonstrate that this conversation will not be an endless emotional appeal, but rather a sincere, and controlled, conversation.

The Tactic: You want to be proactive and put the issue of time on the table.

The Example: "All I want is fifteen minutes of your time, to have this conversation."

One quick word of warning: You must stick to whatever amount of time you establish. I know that's tough, and exceeding those fifteen minutes in this particular case might not be the end of the world. But consider this: You made a deal. You made a deal regarding time, so in a sense, you made a promise. If you want that spouse to trust you and take your conversations seriously, you must keep your promise. With a game plan that involves a whole lot more than pleading for someone to change, you may be surprised at how quickly those fifteen minutes can pass. But regardless of how far you get, a promise is a promise.

For conversations with clients and people you have never met before, this might be the first promise you have ever made. Wouldn't it be a shame if you broke the first promise you ever made?

That said, I see no harm in telling someone, "I promised you that our conversation would last no longer than fifteen minutes, and I want to keep that promise. Would you like to continue this conversation or pick another time when we can meet again to discuss this?" If you are controlling the conversation with your questions, and moving through tactics that are creating both trust and urgency, I think you'll be pleasantly surprised at how many people will surprise you with a desire to continue the conversation.

The bottom line is this: If you can't get a conversation started, nothing else matters. I am not thrilled having to shorten my time either, but for the more difficult conversations, the most important task of all is to get the person you want to influence to agree to meet with you.

WRITE IT OUT

I have never been a fan of scripts; for the most part, they are too constricting. But let me offer an exception to the rule. A lot is riding on the first forty-five seconds of your opening tactic; this is not the time to have to search for your words. Write out your opening and then wordsmith it and practice it. Take a few minutes to choose your words carefully.

I don't recommend taking the paper with those words on it with you into the conversation you are about to have, nor do I recommend memorizing them, exactly. I recommend writing out what you want to say, and practicing it until you're comfortable and natural saying it. If this is a type of conversation you will be having frequently, write out three or four of these openings. This way you'll have a store of phrases you can draw on, and no two openings will sound exactly the same.

AN OPENING FOR ALL OCCASIONS?

There are all kinds of different conversations that involve change, and each can require its own opening. Up until now I've been highlighting an opening to initiate a conversation with someone you have never spoken to before, or broaching a topic you have not spoken about before. Interestingly, the process doesn't really change, but the words do.

For instance, let's say you've had a successful conversation with an individual whose mind *did* change, and an agreement was made to meet at another time to monitor the progress that you've made. Which part of the opening should we drop out?

The introduction? How many times have you met with an individual a second time and not remembered his name, so that you responded to his warm greeting with a resounding, "Hey there, uh . . . buddy!" We're not referring to a close family member in this instance. In business, it never hurts to extend your hand, throw out your name, and slide that card across the table. This action often prompts your client to remind you of his name, which you can then use, to personalize the conversation. So whatever else you do, be sure not to leave sharing your name again out of the conversation.

The hook? What exactly could be the harm in spending a moment explaining to someone the value of meeting again, and monitoring the progress that has been made? If someone was motivated to meet again, I don't think this would discourage her. If she was not motivated to meet again, being reminded of the value of meeting again is not likely to demotivate her. It seems rather obvious, doesn't it, and yet about 90 percent of individuals I've observed in meetings ignore this step thinking it isn't necessary. I think we better keep the hook right where it is.

The process? The same rules apply here. Who wants to sit down in a meeting with another individual having no idea what you really want to do in that meeting? It's a common courtesy to remind someone exactly what you want to accomplish in a meeting, regardless of where this meeting takes place in the *decision cycle*. When influencing another person initially the process may be to ask questions and listen, while later in the *decision cycle* the process may be to explain a solution, or to monitor progress. The words may change, but the act of explaining what will be done in that meeting will not. Nope, I think we better keep the process here, too.

The time? It's a polite thing to do, and quite frankly I don't care where you are in the *decision cycle*, many people appreciate it. It stays.

So you see, no matter where you are in the *decision cycle*, the components remain the same. The words within each stage change, and your success or failure may not weigh quite as heavily as that initial opening, but it would be a mistake to ignore the steps because you are planning a comfortable conversation.

WHEN THE GOING GETS TOUGH

I can't stress enough the importance of a solid tactic to assist you when you need to win those first forty-five seconds and enter into a conversation that requires the changing of another person's mind. The tactic I've outlined represents the best approach possible to begin to initiate change, but, that said, some pretty stubborn situations still require you to dig down a little deeper. In fact, those first forty-five seconds might need to be trimmed even tighter leaving you to struggle with the first few words.

THE FIRST FOUR WORDS

Sometimes when attempting to change another person's mind, the conversation can be a challenging one, and *both* parties know it! Even getting started in those first forty-five seconds can be a little tough. In this case one of the most difficult tasks may very well be finding an effective transition to the opening itself. I've always been a fan of asking for help.

How many times have you sat across from another individual desperately looking for an opportunity to move the conversation in a more challenging direction? Sometimes we wait for an opportunity that will never come. I think you can make this move in a proactive way by using these four simple words.

"I need your help." By beginning your discussion this way, you reduce the feeling of a straight confrontation. In addition, you begin to set the stage for a frank conversation. Finally, taking the element of chance out of the picture, and learning these four words will reduce your anxiety in having the conversation altogether. When there's a lot on the line, I'll take preparation over chance in a heartbeat.

VALUE, NO VALUE

Many salespeople find one of the more difficult challenges to be setting the expectations within a meeting. Often the intentions are so subtle, and the transition to business so difficult, that the results are mixed.

When attempting to engage someone in a conversation that involves change, you must often battle a silent objection to *value*. If the person you want to speak with perceives no value in having a conversation with you, he may lob endless excuses your way. Rather than hope this doesn't occur, or kick the dirt if it does, let's figure a proactive move around it.

I recommend giving a choice to the other person. In fact, I think we should give him two potential outcomes.

"I don't want to tell you what to do, John. I simply want to talk about it, and that means I need to ask questions and listen."

Those choices that follow would sound something like this:

"At the end of our conversation, you will either find value in what we've talked about, or you won't. If you don't find any value, I ask only that you feel comfortable telling me so. I don't want to waste either of our time going over solutions that hold no value to you. Does that sound fair?

On the other hand, if you do find value, and the conversation we are having does make sense, I ask that you... Fair enough?"

On the other hand, if you do find value, and the conversation we are having does make sense, I ask that you truly consider the issues, and we plan a time when we can sit down and talk further about this. Fair enough?

This is a strong tactic because it provides a way out for the person you are trying to communicate with, a reassurance that this conversation will in fact have an ending. I don't recommend this tactic for every conversation, but when you know that getting someone even to sit down and talk with you will be a challenge, this tactic can be extremely effective.

When All Else Fails

I very much enjoy working with wholesalers from the mutual fund industry. These salespeople, among other prospecting activities, frequently move unannounced through the hallways of financial institutions, quickly trying to set up meetings with brokers. The brokers can be a little cantankerous, and are not always receptive to uninvited "drive-by sales calls."

One day, while working for a mutual fund company in the Midwest, one of my wholesaler students asked me a rather interesting question. He wanted to know if I thought a technique he was using was okay. The question, and tactic, went something like this:

> Mr. Jolles, when I go through the hallways knocking on doors, it seems that the toughest offices to get an appointment with are the big brokers. Often, before I can even get a word out I'm told, "Move on! I'm not interested in talking with any wholesalers!" I respond this way: "Fair enough. Please allow me simply to double-check the contact information I have for you, so I can call my home office and

make sure we no longer bother you with any information from our company."

When I asked him what the response was to this exchange he said, "About 99 percent of the time I hear, 'I didn't tell you I don't want any information from your company. I just have no time to meet with you now!' I then ask them when a good time to contact them might be, and more often than not I set an appointment on the spot."

* * *

Clearly, you have to have the right personality to launch into a tactic like that, but I can't argue with this tactic's success. We're *very* close to that manipulation line here, so I'd be careful with a tactic like this, but let's put this exercise through the litmus test regarding influence and manipulation. Is this client better off getting information from this wholesaler, and will the lack of information he has to distribute be a detriment to the client in the long run? I say this tactic stays on the influence side of things, but it is awfully close to that line.

WATCH OUT FOR THOSE BUZZWORDS

Many people create openings with good intentions but they find their success is not improving as dramatically as they would like. Believe it or not, often their lack of success can be tracked to a few harmless buzzwords they don't even realize they're using.

For example, when a salesperson says, "I want to tell you about . . . ," it sounds like he is going to give a lecture to his customer. For an initial call, the salesperson should not "tell you" anything. I would prefer words like, "listen to you."

Buzz Word	*Replace With*
Discuss	Ask
Tell you	Listen to you
Just a few minutes	Fifteen minutes
I need to talk to you	I need your help

Many view the way you begin a discussion as the most crucial part of any conversation. Depending on the scenario, they might be right. A well-thought-out, carefully planned, first forty-five seconds can sure help, a lot. Unfortunately, there is no magic pill. What I do offer, instead, is a sensible approach that provides you with the best opportunity to begin your conversation with an articulate, complete process.

7

"I Object!"

Those who manipulate *see an objection
as a stumbling block to change.*

Those who influence *see an objection as an
opportunity to continue to problem solve.*

M ost people do not naturally study the true potential
of their problems. If they did, not only would
they quickly fix them, but cost would have much less
significance. I've noticed that, regardless of their financial
status, people never look for the least expensive surgeon
when an operation is prescribed; in some cases the issue
of cost has clearly apparent life-altering potential.

Now that you've learned how to influence behavior, all
will be right in your world, right? Let's see.

- Struggling with the ethics involved in influencing
  another's behavior? Done.
- Need to create trust with another person? Done.
- Trying to create a sense of urgency in another person's mind? Done.

That's right; there's nothing like learning about the art
and science behind the human drama of influence. Now

nothing can go wrong. Or can it? Until now, we have been operating in a perfect world, in which everyone we seek to influence cooperates fully. It's now time to upset the apple cart, and see what happens when our processes break down and when those we seek to influence cast aspersions on our perfect world.

WHY PEOPLE OBJECT

I often sense disappointment and fear in the people I work with when they are faced with an objection, but if they had a better understanding of what is making people object, they would be less anxious about hearing these objections. They might also be interested in knowing that the chance of changing someone's mind is reduced by 24 percent when at least one objection is not voiced!

Reason 1: Fear of change

You may not actually hear these words spoken by the person you are trying to convince, but from experience I can tell you: Fear of change permeates just about any decision we make or struggle with. It's instinctive, expected, and quite natural in an individual whose behavior we are trying to influence. After all, it doesn't take a genius to keep things status quo, but to influence behavior, and to move someone from the known to the unknown—that takes courage.

No matter how solid your tactics are, be prepared to face the fear of change in those whom you are influencing. Don't expect them to tell you explicitly that they fear change, but be prepared for some interesting reasons that they choose not to make a change. Unfortunately, this fear of change is often masked by excuses.

We've been working on this fear-of-change issue for a few chapters now, and we've shown that if someone doesn't trust you, there is little chance this person is going to trust you to help him through the fear of change. If someone doesn't feel a sense of urgency, there is little chance this person is going to feel the urgency required to work through the fear of change.

There is a solution, and it comes from your ability to stay away from solving his problem, and to focus instead on leading him to solve his own problems. That means taking those questions you are asking and drilling as deeply as possible into "the pain of the present." If you want to defuse fear of change, it all hinges on your ability to study the problem.

You may hear a rambling story, you may simply hear someone stall, but be prepared to battle this objection giant. Never fear, we'll get around to helping others who are caught in this fear of change, but we have a little more work to do first.

Reason 2: No need

Another classic and common reason people object is that they believe they have no need to change. It sounds simple enough, but it's no accident that this ranks number two among the reasons for objections. The reason behind the objection should no longer appear strange to you because you now know that 79 percent of those struggling with a decision for change do not perceive the issue they are struggling with to be significant enough to warrant a change! Jumping in with a well-intentioned solution simply brings these objections to the surface sooner. The ultimate irony of this particular reason for an objection is that, although it may be a common reason people object, it turns out to be the easiest objection to avoid.

It's amazing what can happen when you set expectations, create trust, and develop a sense of urgency. The proactive approach to working around this issue once again involves the various questioning techniques you have read in the previous chapters. This doesn't mean you won't have to address a "no need" objection. It does mean, however, that the better job you have done to set the stage earlier in the conversation, the less frequently you will be faced with this objection.

Reason 3: No hurry

A frustrating complaint that is often brought up in my seminars is one with which you are probably very familiar. It goes something like this:

> Frequently I sit down with my son and everything seems to be going fine. I make a couple of simple suggestions, and I'm greeted with some favorable head nods. Then the conversation turns to *when* he will do what I'm asking him to do, and everything comes to a screeching halt.

Sound familiar? The person you are looking to influence might offer any number of excuses, but make no mistake about it: You are looking at a "no hurry" objection. What makes it so frustrating is that most people will swear they had the situation locked up and in the bag before the objection is made. Well, that bag has sprung a leak.

The reason I have strongly encouraged you to stay on a particular problem and ask second- and third-level questions regarding that problem is that this is where urgency lies. Our success does not lie in how passionately we express a solution, but rather in our more methodical effort to study the problem. "So let's figure out what we're going to do when, because the fear of change, exasperated by no perceived need or hurry, will strengthen someone's resolve to still say no."

THE CASE OF THE MANAGEMENT MESS

Handling Objections

Background: You have been managing a new employee for about six months now. She is a workhorse, and will attack every task given to her with everything she has. However, when she joined your team you were told she had a history of not getting along well with others. Unfortunately, you had no idea how serious this issue was and it's beginning to disrupt your entire team.

The Tactic: You want this employee to become more comfortable in group situations, so you attempted to convince her to attend an offsite training program to address this particular issue.

FOUR STEPS TO HANDLING OBJECTIONS

Many people feel that there is some deep, dark mystery to handling objections. Well, I hope you have learned that if there is a secret, it lies in your proactive approach to understanding how people make decisions, and intelligently mirroring their process to influence behavior. Still, if there is a secret to handling objections, you'll find it sitting in step one.

Step 1: Clarify

The first, and by far the most important, step within the *objection-handling* tactic is to *clarify* the objection. Do not be deceived by what appears to be a simple step. Clarification can be a challenge because it requires you to think quickly on your feet. Still, it's the most important step, and here are three reasons (among others) to do it:

Reason 1: Get at the *Real* Objection. Rarely will people give their real objection right up front. Maybe it's embarrassing, maybe they feel it's personal, or maybe it's because they don't think it's as important as you think it is. One thing is certain: When you get at the real objection, you can address the real objection, and asking someone to clarify her concern will do just that.

I can't begin to tell you how many times I have personally jumped to my favorite response regarding an issue that had nothing to do with the question being asked because I didn't get at the real objection. By the time I finished answering the question that was never asked, I was rewarded by having to fend off the objection I had now created. What a mess!

Reason 2: Avoid Sounding Confrontational. Here's a strange irony for you: Let's say you guess right and actually *do* understand the real objection without clarifying it first. Your potential reward will not be a compliment for your clairvoyant talents. Your reward will be annoyance regarding your confrontational, stubborn, and insensitive approach to communication. So instead of sounding confrontational, set the stage for understanding. Not only will you buy yourself time to think, by clarifying the objection that comes your way, you will be sending an important message regarding your intention to listen and understand.

Reason 3: Avoid Talking Too Much. Picture yourself in the other person's shoes for just a moment. You are looking at a rather difficult decision and trying to analyze that decision as carefully as possible. You are puzzled by one aspect of this decision, so you pose a rather harmless question to ask the person to help you understand something. Out comes a response that just won't end. It goes on and on and on. You begin thinking to yourself, "This was really not such a big deal to me a minute ago, but judging by this person's response, I must have hit on a bigger problem than I thought!"

The longer it take a person to answer an objection verbally, the more credibility the objection is given.

In other words, your inability to understand the objection, which you demonstrate by providing a boatload of information in which the answer is somewhere buried, dramatically damages your credibility. I've always been fond of this proverb to remind me of this message: "That which proves too much, proves nothing."

If I still haven't been able to convince you of the importance of clarifying, let me put it to you simply: One out of ten objections isn't even an objection, and that's a conservative number. What you are really hearing is someone who does not want to be influenced and who is stalling. If you ask that person to *clarify* the objection, don't be surprised to hear, "Uh, well, you see, I think you actually answered that question earlier." That's because there is no objection!

THE CASE OF THE MANAGEMENT MESS

Clarifying

The Need: Rather than creating an objection that doesn't exist, sounding confrontational, or losing control of the conversation, you want to delve deeper into the issue.

The Tactic: You need to *clarify* the objection.

The Exchange: The conversation might sound something like this:

Employee: "I don't really think I need to attend any outside training for this issue."

Employer: "What specifically concerns you about the training program?"

Employee: "I told you I'd address this problem. I just don't think an outside program is going to fix this. I have to fix this. I just don't want to make a fool of myself."

Employer: "So, if I hear you correctly, your real concern is the sensitivity, or in some cases, the lack of sensitivity that can be shown in programs like this. Is that correct?"

Employee: "Yes."

You don't want to antagonize the other person, or to put her on the spot, so be prepared to assist her out of her predicament gracefully. It might be helpful to make a comment about how confusing her topic is. However, I would rather help someone feel comfortable moving away from an attempt at stalling than to breathe life into an objection that does not exist.

Step 2: Acknowledge

Assuming the objection has been clarified, it's time to demonstrate your listening skills. It may be time to demonstrate your empathy skills as well. *Acknowledging* another person's objection means it's time for you to confirm your understanding of this person's concern. When you acknowledge, what you're really doing is demonstrating your understanding of the objection. Clarifying may help get you to the right objection. Acknowledging will confirm it for you. An example of the first two steps might sound something like this.

THE CASE OF THE MANAGEMENT MESS

Acknowledging

The Need: You want to be sensitive with a person who has opened up a bit, and trusted you with the real reason for her hesitancy.

The Tactic: You need to show empathy as you *acknowledge* the objection.

The Exchange: The conversation might sound something like this:

Employer: "I can certainly understand your hesitancy. I've been to some training programs that don't exactly model sensitivity. I want you to know I have not only personally attended this program, I know the trainer who teaches it. I can assure you, I would not send you to a program in which I did not have full confidence not only about what is taught but about how it is taught."

Step 3: Respond

Assuming you now know what the real objection is, and you have acknowledged it, it's time to *respond*. However, to do this effectively, we need to figure out what type of objection you are responding to. Then we'll be all set to answer it. Fortunately, there are only two real types of objections. We'll cover the easier one first.

MISUNDERSTANDINGS

Ah, wouldn't life be grand if all objections were misunderstandings? A misunderstanding objection means just that: The person you are communicating with has misunderstood something, so you need to clear it up. The solution is fairly simple, but not without an element of risk. In fact, it's often a classic case of not *what* you say, but *how* you say it.

The goal here is not to fall into the trap of making yourself "right" and the other person "wrong." The goal here is tactfully to remove an impending obstacle of personal ego, and get back on track to influencing behavior.

"Feel, Felt, Found"

I would like to suggest a technique I have admired and used for years. I refer to it as "feel, felt, found," and when it comes to gracefully telling someone she is wrong, it works like a charm.

The *feel* portion of this technique is designed to deflect the ego that's often in the way here. When you tell someone that a lot of people *feel* the same way she does, you immediately avoid the risk of putting that person in a defensive position.

The *felt* portion of this technique injects empathy into your response. It's one thing for someone to hear that a lot of people *feel* the same way she does. However, it's much more powerful for that person to hear that *you* felt the same way yourself!

The *found* portion of this technique provides your response. At this point the answer should be an easy one, but there is no sense dropping the ball here. By explaining what you have *found*, you open the way to offer your answer with the least amount of confrontation. Let's hear this technique in action and pick up where we left off from the previous example.

THE CASE OF THE MANAGEMENT MESS

Feel, Felt, Found

The Need: Faced with an objection that is really more of a misunderstanding, you do not want the person you are communicating with to feel as if she is wrong.

The Tactic: You need to avoid bruising her ego, show empathy, and correct this misunderstanding.

The Exchange: The conversation might sound something like this:

Employer: "I can assure you, I would not send you to a program in which I did not have full confidence not only about what is taught but about how it is taught."

Employee: "Okay, but I'm still not sure I do well in these kinds of programs. You never know what the other attendees will be like. I've seen programs like this ruined by a few insensitive people."

Employer: "You know, a lot of people *feel* the same way you do when they attend a program like this. It can be a bit intimidating, and you never know who else will be attending. I *felt* the same way, too, when I went through this program. I thought, 'I really want to get something out of this. What if others in attendance aren't taking this as seriously as I am?' But what I *found* was when you have a good, solid curriculum and a great trainer running it, you don't have to worry about the other attendees."

Using the "feel, felt, found" technique allows you to tell someone, gracefully, that she is wrong. I would be careful not to use this technique more than once per conversation, and don't worry if you don't incorporate all three parts of the process. It's a guide, and nothing more, but you will be amazed at how often it gets you out of a sticky situation!

DRAWBACK

The most difficult type of objection to handle is the drawback objection. An objection due to a drawback really means that there is a particular element of the argument you *cannot* address! Fear not, though, because where there's a will, there's a way!

First, let's put this in perspective. The last time you bought a car, did you get everything you wanted? Oh, I'm quite sure you got the color or the style, but unless you ordered that car, and had it custom constructed just for you, I'm guessing it only had *almost* everything you were looking for.

You see, much like your car, or your job, or you house, or your spouse (okay, maybe not your spouse), I believe you made your decision based on the issue as a whole, not on only one or two pieces of that issue. If you believe that the decision you are influencing is truly in the best interest of the person you are persuading, stay strong, and push on! After you have clarified and acknowledged, I suggest you put things in perspective and summarize the benefits of the solution you're driving toward.

THE CASE OF THE MANAGEMENT MESS

Drawback

The Need: Faced with an objection that presents a shortcoming to your position, you want to help the person you are communicating with gain perspective on the situation.

The Tactic: You want to minimize this issue and focus on the solution as a whole.

The Exchange: The conversation might sound something like this:

Employer: "But what I *found* was when you have a good, solid curriculum and a great trainer running it, you don't have to worry about the other attendees."

Employee: "Okay, it sounds like a good program. But I don't want to give up one of my weekends to attend it."

Employer: "Unfortunately, the only time this program is held is over the weekend, to accommodate those who cannot attend during regular working hours. However, ask yourself what's most important to you overall—a program that addresses your single biggest development issue, in a supportive environment, or giving up one day of your weekend to attend it?"

If, by chance, you are wondering where these other benefits to your solution magically come from, please remember the lessons you have learned up to this point. Remember that rather than tell someone what she should be doing, you created trust, and you created urgency around the other benefits of your solution. It was *you* who created perspective!

The only gentle reminder I would like to offer once again involves ethics. If the solution you are proposing does not address the other person's most important criteria, you have to think seriously about what you are influencing her to do. The idea here is to gain perspective regarding this drawback, not to convince someone it isn't necessary. We're at a pretty important fork in the road here when it comes to influence *without* manipulation.

Those who manipulate *restate benefits to convince others a drawback to their solution isn't necessary.*

Those who influence *restate benefits to help others gain perspective on their solution as a whole.*

Step 4: Confirm

Have you ever heard an objection that just did not seem to want to go away? You have responded to the objection, moved on, and, *boom*, it rears its ugly head once again. Sometimes objections can take on a life of their own, turning up over and over again, like a bad penny. Each time you think you have satisfied the objection with a good answer, ten minutes later you hear, "I'm still hung up on . . ."

The best way to handle this problem is to confirm that the person's objection has been addressed.

THE CASE OF THE MANAGEMENT MESS

Confirming

The Need: Faced with an objection that presents a shortcoming to your position, you want to help the person you are communicating with gain perspective of the situation.

The Tactic: You've worked hard to address this objection, and now it's time to put it to bed.

The Exchange: The conversation might sound something like this:

Employer: "What's most important to you overall—a program that addresses your single biggest development issue, in a supportive environment, or giving up one day of your weekend to attend it?"

Employee: "I see your point."

Employer: "Great, then you're ready to tackle this?"

Employee: "Well, if I'm going to do it, I might as well do it now. Sign me up."

Often simply, "How does that sound?" or even "Okay?" will do the trick. The key is to try and get the person you are working with to tell you that her objection has been adequately addressed. Once you have asked this question, you can count on one of two responses. She either will or will not be satisfied with the way you've handled her objection. If she is not satisfied, you might as well know now before you move on. I would suggest more clarification and possibly a return visit to the questions that brought you here in the first place.

I believe that the confirmation step is almost as important as the clarification step. Still, if you listen hard enough, you will find that, on many occasions, the person you are talking with will confirm her responses to objections for you. It's not uncommon to hear people say things like, "I really like that" or "That sounds great." Needless to say, in situations like these, the confirmation step has already been accomplished for you. After someone has said, "That sounds great," it would be awkward to say, "Uh, so does that address your concern?"

Now, I will not for a minute tell you that by confirming your response to the objection, you have guaranteed the objection will not be heard again. What I *can* tell you is that by confirming, you have psychologically made it much more difficult for the objection to be brought up again.

Sometimes an objection can be perceived simply as a question. And sometimes when people have a simple question, it can be perceived as an objection.

You could try to determine which it is by studying nonverbal cues, emotional expression, and other difficult signals to pick up, but I think this will only confuse the issue more. I have a better idea. Why not treat both objections and questions the same way?

When you are asked a question, doesn't it make sense to *clarify* the question to make sure you understand it, and confirm it has been answered when you have finished addressing it? When you treat perceived objections and questions the same way, you no longer have to worry about misreading someone's intent.

Oscar Wilde once wrote, "Experience is the name everyone gives to their mistakes." Sometimes when dealing with various challenging situations and objections, it's safe to say that you'll be gaining some experience from time to time.

Sorry seems to be the hardest word, and the most ineffective.

All of us make mistakes. Sometimes when you are truly seeking information, and clarifying objections, you may gain a different perspective regarding the argument you thought you were making. In short, you may find that you were wrong. Take a deep breath, because here comes the most toxic word and most common mistake you can make when faced with a scenario like this. The mistake is to trust your instincts and to apologize.

It is a natural tendency to want to say "I'm sorry" to someone when you have let him or her down. Don't get me wrong—I have no problem apologizing to my wife or to my friends when I have been at fault, and I would be happy to recommend you use these words in business if they were of any use. Unfortunately, they are not. Telling a customer you are sorry is the equivalent of waving a red cloth in front of a bull. It only makes things worse.

One of the reasons the word "sorry" is of such little use when dealing with challenging situations is that usually the problem you are apologizing for is not your mistake, and the customer knows it. Did you personally create the worldwide economic crisis? Did you personally underwrite questionable loans or create the banking crisis? To the customer, the word "sorry" represents an empty, useless word that can sometimes even appear to be more condescending than sincere. Used insincerely, the word "sorry" can feel just as hollow in a close relationship. People don't want you to be sorry. People want their concerns to be acknowledged, and they want to be listened to.

The next time you hear someone complain about an issue involving you or your company, let this person know you have heard him by simply saying, "I can understand your frustration" or "I can certainly appreciate how disappointing that must be." This acknowledges the other person's concerns. Then restate the issue. "You placed a lot of income and faith in a market that has provided an enormous amount of volatility." This demonstrates that you have been listening. It also demonstrates empathy, which is critical here. Now you can begin to address the real concern.

I cannot guarantee that if you follow this process an irate person will magically be happy with the realities of his current situation. What I can tell you, based on years of using this process and teaching it to thousands of others, is that it will dramatically help to defuse the emotion. The rest is up to you. Once this emotion has been defused, it is safe to ask your questions, and it will be up to you to reestablish trust, problem solve, and listen. This will allow you to lead the person you are communicating with to a new solution, and perhaps even to a deeper relationship with you.

THE ULTIMATE NEMESIS: "IT COSTS TOO MUCH!"

When I give a seminar, probably the most frequently asked questions center around how to address objections dealing with price. Specifically, what do you do when someone says, "It costs too much!" The answer is found in a three-letter acronym called "TCO," which stands for Total Cost of Ownership. It's human nature to look at a solution, particularly a premium-priced solution, and balk at its cost. Who wants to buy an eighty-dollar electric toothbrush when there's a ten-dollar toothbrush sitting right next to it? Your dentist, for one, and your teeth, for another. You can walk out of that store feeling like you just kept seventy dollars in your pocket, but did you really find the least expensive solution?

My "Brush" with TCO

Peggy, my dental hygienist for years has had me on the straight and narrow path, and Peggy doesn't lie. Yes, people can spend a whole lot longer with that manual toothbrush and get the job done, but do they? The experts like Peggy say no.

That eighty-dollar toothbrush you left in the aisle will stroke your teeth 400 times faster than your manual toothbrush. Most electric toothbrushes provide you with a two-minute timer, coincidentally exactly what the American Dental Association recommends for time spent brushing. Suffice it to say, I think it's not too hard for Peggy to prove you will be brushing a whole lot more effectively with that toothbrush that "costs too much." But let's keep running the numbers here.

Before I got my electric toothbrush, I went in every six months for a cleaning. Now it's every nine months because my teeth are cleaner.

Forget the part about me having a cleaner mouth, reduced risk for gum disease, and perhaps even a more professional appearance. Do you still think that manual toothbrush would have saved me money?

✳ ✳ ✳

When moving someone to a TCO conversation, the question is a simple one: "When you say it costs too much, are you referring to the cost of buying it, or the cost of owning it?" Be prepared to see a slightly confused expression, and to hear the words, "I don't understand the difference."

That's when you can spring into action and help someone understand the total cost of ownership. The key is to get those who are objecting to look at the *total* picture of a solution they are considering. It doesn't matter if it's a tangible, or an intangible, solution.

Over the years I've put this concept in place with solutions as obvious as a Xerox copier salesman selling copy quality and as obscure as a polygraph examiner selling the truth. Cost is an objection that should not surprise anyone, and being distracted from considering total costs is the norm, not the exception. In the absence of value, cost will always be the most important criteria in another person's mind. It's our job to get people to look at total costs, be it monetary, experiential, or emotional.

8

How to Change
Your Mind

Those who manipulate *struggle with implementation,
seeing the mastering of these skills as something
they will revisit when it serves them.*

Those who influence *dedicate themselves to
implementation, seeing the mastering of these skills
as a way to help others in need of change.*

Now that we have our process for changing minds
clearly defined and on the table, it would appear that
our job is done. We've touched all the bases. You have seen
why people often avoid change and need assistance when
it comes to modifying various habits. You have looked at
the inside of the minds of those who struggle with change,
and studied why they struggle, and even when they tend
to struggle. You have examined a process to create trust,
the blueprint for change, and a process to create urgency.
You have learned how to begin the conversation, how to
finish the conversation, and how to handle conflict within
the conversation. But our work is still not done.

In my thirty-plus years of working with audiences,
it has always puzzled me why so many people eagerly
buy into concepts and processes, but in the end fail to

implement them. Well, I think I know the answer, and I'd like to solve this mystery right now. In the words of Walt Kelly, "We have met the enemy and he is us."

We must stop thinking that when a process is taught, it somehow becomes more of a straitjacket than a process. This can come from an overzealous teacher, or perhaps even an author with just a little *too* much passion. Your success in using these, or any processes you learn, is not dependent only on your ability to memorize them. In fact, just as important, if not more important, is your ability to apply these processes to each unique situation that arises. One size definitely does *not* fit all.

The ultimate test of any process to influence behavior is its ability to expand and contract to any persuasive situation.

I am not suggesting that processes aren't critical to our success. I'm merely saying that these processes represent nothing more than a guide. These, and other processes like them, must be flexible and provide the user with the option to sift through what may be needed, and what is not. In the end we must remember that people make decisions, not processes. This is where what I refer to as *strategic decision-making* comes in.

A STRATEGIC CHECKLIST

Up to this point, you have been kind enough to let me methodically walk you through the steps necessary to *change minds.* Now let's mess things up a bit, suspend disbelief, and pretend that not everyone to whom we are applying these skills follows the steps exactly as they have been laid out. Allow me take you through a checklist that will help guide you in determining how to apply this process to various situations. Each question has the potential to affect the strategies you will employ and to provide you with a better idea of how to let this process expand and contract around your unique situations.

Where is the Person You are Influencing in His or Her Decision Cycle? To me, no strategic decision can be made until you know where the other is in *his or her decision cycle.* This is the first domino that must fall before you can make any other decisions; therefore, it is more like a mantra than a step within a process. It all begins here. Listen for cues that would identify where the person you are communicating with may be in his or her *decision cycle.*

Does the person you are communicating with want to make a change or not? If you are going to make an error, I would suggest you err on the side of caution. In other words, when in doubt, move backward and not forward in the *decision cycle* and your choice of tactics.

What Steps Would Be Most Critical? If you want to *change minds,* you're going to need a game plan. Within that game plan, you will call on various tactics. The obvious question then becomes, "What steps within this process will I need?"

Sometimes the clues are clear as to where another person is in his or her *decision cycle*, making the tactics clear as well. Other times it might require a few careful questions that will provide a temperature read into the minds of those you intend to change. Once the tactics have been chosen, another domino has fallen as well.

What Steps Would Be Least Critical? No steps within this, or any process, are cast in stone, but instead represent a series of conscious choices based on information at hand. I know you have heard these words from me often, but let's say them one last time. The main tactics outlined in this book represent a process, and nothing more. They are not intended to constrict anyone's behavior; instead, they are meant to be flexible. Once we determine where someone is in his or her *decision cycle*, certain steps within the process will be more important than others. In other words, despite how passionate I might be in explaining key tactics, sometimes key tactics just aren't necessary.

Pause and consider these words again: "Sometimes key tactics just *aren't* necessary." These words are coming from this author straight to you. The author is telling you *not* to use all the steps he just taught you. That might make me a lousy author, but it makes for one heck of an honest one! I can assure you, I would not have created each and every step within this process if I didn't think it was important. However, when we deal with the real world, we find that different steps become more or less critical based on many factors, including personality, geographic location, and where someone is in his or her *decision cycle,* to mention a few. And that means constructing a conversation that fits the scenario within which you are working.

Trust, for example, and the steps contained within that stage of the process, are critical. But what if the scenario you are working within brings you face to face with someone you know well? It would be annoying and clumsy to ask that person basic questions that you already know. Imagine beginning a conversation with one of your best clients, with whom you have worked for years, with a question like, "Can you tell me about yourself?"

The funny thing is, not only do I think it's okay to dismiss certain steps within this or any process, I think it's imperative. I'm such a believer in tailoring this approach to the real world that a few years ago I changed every program my company delivers to reflect this approach. Of course, I still have people role-play within the programs we teach, but we also have them participate in case studies and simulations that allow students to shuffle through the tactics to mimic the real world more accurately.

What Are Some Anticipated Strengths and Weaknesses of Your Position? Understanding the strengths of your position can provide a lot of help when determining what questions to ask, and where you might lead someone through your conversation. Understanding the weaknesses of your position can often be even *more* helpful.

Analyzing your potential weaknesses will give you a head start on issues that should not be avoided. Your frank and honest acceptance of the weaknesses in your position may help set an honest tone to the conversation, and even create the right atmosphere for potential compromise. It may also help prepare you for potential objections that you may be faced with, as well as strategies for how to deal with those objections.

When you learn how to change minds, you learn that no solution is a perfect solution. There are strengths and weaknesses to every position. Using the proper skills to draw another person to the strengths of your solution, and also accepting the weaknesses, can go a long way to influence, without manipulation.

Those who manipulate *focus exclusively on the strengths of their position.*

Those who influence *focus and analyze both the strengths and weaknesses of their position.*

What Objections Do You Anticipate Hearing?
Sometimes it is hard to anticipate which objections you will hear, and other times these objections are no surprise at all. Rather than hoping you will not have to deal with an anticipated objection, why not prepare for it?

Study your position. Study the position of the person whose mind you are attempting to change through influence. What are the typical objections you can count on hearing? Is there a trust issue? Is there a fear of change issue? Is there an ego issue, an urgency issue, or an issue of denial?

You have already learned how to handle objections, so I will not restate the process here. Instead, I will suggest that you write out some clarification questions along with some well-worded responses. This should give you confidence and provide you with articulate, nondefensive responses to potential objections.

What Opening Adjustments Will You Make? The opening is another critical element of your strategic decision-making. Sometimes this opening represents the first words out of your mouth, and other times it represents a much-needed transition from a comfortable conversation to a potentially uncomfortable confrontation.

The key, once again, is *preparation*. Study your opening, and based on what you know about the person you are meeting, try to anticipate the adjustments you'll have to make. If this represents an important conversation to you, I suggest you write out that opening in advance. I've always recommended creating a handful of openings so that you can mix and match key phrases on the fly. This will allow you to put your best foot forward even if you are forced on the spot to make strategic decisions regarding your opening. This preparation will position you strategically to win the first battle you face—those all-important first forty-five seconds.

What Personality Adjustments Will You Make? Everything you've read so far is a vital part of this handy checklist, but this final element will help provide a better sense of pace. When do you transition with that opening, and how long do you spend with those questions designed to establish trust? Just how hard do you hit someone with the more difficult questions that can create pain, and how long do you stay there? It often becomes a matter of personality.

I'm all for the intricate personality processes that exist, but in the world of fast-paced, on-the-spot interactions, these reads and adjustments must be lightning fast. In fact, I think it will all boil down to one of three personalities you will face when learning how to change minds—*dominant, analytical,* and *social.*

If a person is demonstrating *dominant* tendencies:

- You'll see it in her clothes, which are often somewhat conservative.
- You'll see it in her home, or office, which will be somewhat barren.
- You'll see it in her emails, which are short, and not particularly—well—friendly.
- You'll hear it in her speech, which will be somewhat—well—to the point.

Quite frankly, you'll need to speed up and get to your point. The world of schmoozing is lost on this personality type. Get that opening going, get to your point, and move briskly through the tactics. Dominant people are potentially the most aggressive to work with. But they'll also be the quickest to take action if the solution you are drawing them to makes sense. If you keep your ears open, and listen for signals that reflect a willingness to move forward, you'll change the dominant personality's mind.

If a person is demonstrating *analytical* tendencies:

- You'll see it in his clothes, which are also somewhat conservative.

- You'll see it in his home or office, which will be somewhat cluttered but orderly.

- You'll see it in his emails, which will be somewhat orderly and to the point.

- You'll hear it in his speech, which will be detailed and deliberate.

Now you'll need to come armed with facts and figures, and not feelings. Sharing how you "feel" about an idea is lost on him; providing him real data to support your idea is not. Stick to the logic behind the conversation you are having by letting him know you want to understand things from his side of the issue, and understand more about the challenges of his situation. If you can "prove" your case, you'll change the analytical personality's mind.

If a person is demonstrating social tendencies:

- You'll see it in her clothes, which will be a little bit more colorful and adventurous.

- You'll see it in her home or office, which will be somewhat messy with a lot of pictures on the wall.

- You'll see it in her emails, which will be loaded with a LOT of social comments and creativity.

- You'll hear it in her speech, which you'll have no trouble hearing because it will go on and on.

With these personality types, you'll need to let them go on and possibly ramble a bit instead of rushing into your part of the conversation. Pushing them to the point too fast will be perceived as rude. The good news is these personalities will be the easiest to get to the table for a conversation. The bad news is they will typically be the most difficult influence. This isn't because they won't agree with most of the changes you suggest. It's because they will avoid actually *acting* on the change they've agreed to. There is no personality that needs more discipline in following through on the tactics selected, particularly the tactics that create urgency. If you avoid taking the bait and rushing away from the questions that create pain, you'll change the social personality's mind.

That's a rather quick jaunt through the world of personality, but it not only belongs on our checklist, it provides a little perspective to the speed of the tactics needed when you learn how to change minds as well. It may be logical, but it took me about a decade to accept personality as a criterion of influence.

IT'S NOT ABOUT ME;
IT'S ABOUT YOU

It's a little embarrassing to admit, but I was never fond of the various personality processes that appeared over the years. These were the programs that identified various personality types and provided insight into the things about yourself that you never quite understood before.

For a period of time, it seemed as if every company I worked with was investing in these programs to help them sell more effectively. After all, once you went through this extensive, multipage assessment, you had a pretty accurate understanding of what motivates you, what demotivates you, how you want to be managed, strengths and weaknesses of selling, and much, much more.

Personally, I fought these programs for one stubborn reason: I felt the information I was gaining from these assessments was absolutely perfect, as long as I was selling to *me* for the rest of my life! I always felt the information was aimed at the wrong person. I'm as interested as the next guy to learn more about myself, and be a better person, but, quite frankly, I didn't want this to be about me. I wanted it to be about the person sitting across from me.

So I treated these programs with disdain, often claiming: "Who needs them?" I can't go to my clients and say, "Uh, pardon me, would you mind taking this assessment so I can figure out how to sell to you more effectively?" In my book, this conversation about personality had no business in the trenches with real sales training. It was insulting to me that these processes even dared to try to pass themselves off as sales processes!

And then I realized I was wrong. So often, when I fielded questions from audience members, I heard things like: "How long should I spend chitchatting with a client before I move into the business side of things?" Wouldn't that depend on the personality of the client?

The fact is that I needed those personality processes, and I appreciated their attention to learning more about individual human behavior. But the personality processes needed more attention to skills that taught true selling techniques as well.

Full personality assessments are great as management tools, and wonderful to show family and friends at parties, but they won't be a lot of help when you are training your eyes on someone else you are meeting for the first time. What will work is studying how someone dresses, how an office or home environment is set up, or even learning to read personality from emails and voicemails. These kinds of reads will give you a head start, and your early questions will allow you to fine-tune your assessment.

In the real world, many personality reads are made on the fly, so it's extremely difficult to juggle the level of detail in multilevel assessments. You don't need such in-depth assessments. The three personality types we've discussed—dominant, analytical, social will cover all the bases for you.

Our instinctive behavior is to try to communicate with people with whom we feel naturally comfortable: people who are like us. Unfortunately, when you are trying to persuade someone else, it's *his or her* personality that matters, and that means communicating in the way that he or she would like to be communicated with.

AND FINALLY

The system of influence that I teach is not a pamphlet with a few good ideas; it is a *process*. When you try to perfect any process, it requires a commitment to implement what has been learned. This means leaving the comfort confines of the status quo and venturing into new ideas and new tactics. For many, the challenge is to avoid slipping back into old, comfortable tactics, especially when faced with a live human being uncomfortably staring you down. But when you believe that change is necessary, are there any real alternatives?

When you don't know where a person is in his or her *decision cycle*, or what repeatable steps would be necessary to *change minds* logically, the focus falls on one thing only: Did you convince him or her, or not? Did you win, or did you lose? To evaluate your performance solely on whether you influenced change or not falls somewhere between naive and ignorant. What about the peace of mind you gain knowing that you put together the most intelligent, structured approach to persuasion you could possibly have designed?

One of the biggest challenges is the temptation to push someone into a decision rather than take the time and effort necessary to change another person's mind. However, an even bigger test will be to know when to dig in and fight, and when the fight is not in the best interest of those whose minds you seek to change. It doesn't *have* to be about winning or losing.

Is Winning the Only Thing?

While I was growing up, I was a fan of the late Vince Lombardi. Not only was he one of the greatest coaches ever, but he also finished his career with my Washington Redskins. He is the man who is forever linked to the following words: "Winning isn't everything; it's the only thing."

There is an irony to this: Lombardi isn't the one who came up with that quote, nor did he mean it when he said it. For the record, the quote was actually attributed to Henry "Red" Sanders, the football coach for the UCLA Bruins in 1950. In 1959, Lombardi used the line to open the Packers training camp. According to the late James Michener's *Sports in America*, Lombardi claimed to have been misquoted. What he intended to say was this:"Winning isn't everything. The will to win is the only thing."

That certainly changes the intent of that quote, doesn't it? It also gives you a little more insight into the nature of Lombardi. Look at that quote again. Lombardi, one of the most competitive and successful coaches in professional sports history, was really telling us something else: He was saying "effort is what ultimately defines success." This is an important distinction because I think we often define our success by counting our victories.

Those who know me well consider me to be an intense person, both inside and out. You may be surprised to know, however, that throughout my professional career, my reaction to either winning or losing has never been that different. As a young salesman, when I made a nice sale, I would celebrate with a bag of barbecued potato chips. That bag of chips symbolized victory.

But that wasn't the only time I rewarded myself with that bag of chips. When I worked hard on a sale by taking no short-cuts, by sticking to my process, and by giving it my all, I'd eat those chips even if I didn't make the sale. It was a struggle at first because I never wanted to get into a habit of rewarding failure. But I wasn't rewarding failure; I was rewarding effort.

To this day, I can forgive a professional loss, but what I can't forgive is a loss knowing I didn't do all I could to be successful.

✳ ✳ ✳

We learned this as children and were allowed to define success by our effort and our will to win. Much like Lombardi's quote that took on a life of its own, so has the flawed concept that success should be defined solely by winning. Is it any wonder that so many people struggle in life with depression and the fear of failure? Personally, I believe this is a direct result of people elevating the act of winning to a life-and-death equation.

North Carolina's Dean Smith, one of the most successful college basketball coaches in the history of the sport (coming from a Maryland Terrapin alumnus, that's not easy for me to admit), said it best when he provided us with this thought: "If you make every game a life and death proposition, you're going to have problems. For one thing, you'll be dead a lot."

Let's pay tribute to both Dean Smith and Vince Lombardi, and remember both men for the real messages they gave us. If we do, we can set goals and achieve results that are 100 percent controlled by our effort . . . just as we did when we were children. I think we would all be a lot happier with ourselves if we did this—don't you?

Those who manipulate *define victory solely by the change they create.*

Those who influence *define victory by the ethical effort they put forth in their attempts to bring about change.*

I wish you well in your quest to *change minds*. It will require trial and error. It will involve success and failure. My hope is that through these pages you've found a simple, well-thought-out approach to maximizing your efforts to influence others ethically and empathetically. That also means defining success, not by the minds you change, but by your absolute best effort to understand and apply the tactics you've learned. At the end of the day, that's all you can ask for.

Perfect your tactics, use your checklist, and trust your instincts. Before you know it, you'll be able not only to *change minds*, but to do so by applying the *art of influence without manipulation*. Most important, never, *ever* question the importance of what you are doing for others when you guide them to change.

Who Am I?

A "Sto-em" by Rob Jolles

A "STO-EM"

I prevent financial tragedies every time I get you to finally believe that your retirement and children's education are more important than a seven-day cruise.

* * *

I save lives every time I get you to stop putting off "what if" and purchase an item that protects you and your loved ones.

* * *

I assist you each time I am able to get you to look past your decisions of the moment, and instead look at the "big picture" of your decisions in the future.

• • •

I'm the person in the store. You felt put off by all my questions but wound up with a solution that not only saved your business that day, but also saved your job a year later as my product expanded along with your business.

• • •

I'm the person who changed your mind about skimping on a business expenditure that was later responsible for bringing you your biggest customer.

• • •

I looked you in the eye and asked you some disturbing questions. It upset you, but your anger toward me saved your life and the lives of others on a road you would have been too drunk to drive on.

• • •

I put up with the stereotypical fallacies that have portrayed me in a less than positive light; in actuality, I was the only one who provided for the future of your family when an early death might have meant devastating and dramatic changes in your loved ones' worlds.

• • •

I could have taken no for an answer, and sometimes I wish I had. I could not because I had seen the personal tragedy of procrastination.

• • •

I have empathy for your fear of change because I have similar fears. The fear of the unknown often outweighs the pain of the present. I have shown up to move you past these fears and get you to take action in an ethical manner.

• • •

I may not be apparent to all, but I exist in everyone's soul.

• • •

Who am I? I am the person who will change your mind, and I'll do so using the *art of influence without manipulation.*

How to Change Minds
Worksheet

☐ Where is the person you are influencing in his or her decision cycle?

☐ What steps would be most critical?

☐ What steps would be least critical?

☐ What are some anticipated strengths and weaknesses of your position?

☐ What objections do you anticipate hearing?

☐ What personality adjustments will you make?

Opening Notes: _____

_____

_____

_____

_____

_____

_____

Appendix

Influence without Manipulation

At its core, when you are applying influence and changing another person's mind, you are taking an idea, planting that idea in his brain, and making him feel as if he thought of it.

• • •

Those who *manipulate* engage in persuasion regardless of their personal feelings about a solution.

Those who *influence* engage in persuasion only if their personal feelings support their solution.

• • •

Those who *manipulate* obsess on persuasive tactics they can follow.

Those who *influence* obsess on understanding the decision process followed by those they are persuading.

• • •

Those who *manipulate* don't ask for trust.

Those who *influence* don't need to ask for trust; they earn it.

• • •

Those who *manipulate* put their faith in the right argument.

Those who *influence* put their faith in the right question.

• • •

Those who *manipulate* tell others about their problems.

Those who *influence* allow others to tell them about their problems.

• • •

Those who *manipulate* "push" a person through his statements, telling him about a problem that may exist.

Those who *influence* "push" a person through his questions, allowing that person to discover the potential of a problem that may exist.

• • •

Those who *manipulate* passionately explain the impact of not acting on their recommendation.

Those who *influence* compassionately listen to another person explain in his or her own words the impact of not acting to solve an existing problem.

• • •

Those who *manipulate* inadvertently display a sense of satisfaction when hearing of another person's pain. It represents a personal triumph.

Those who *influence* display empathy when hearing of another person's pain. It represents trust, and they too feel that pain.

• • •

Those who *manipulate* believe the more you ask for a commitment, the greater your chances of success.

Those who *influence* believe you earn the right to ask for someone's commitment.

• • •

Those who *manipulate* see an opening as a way to mislead someone into engaging in a conversation.

Those who *influence* see an opening as a way to determine if there are mutual benefits in engaging in a conversation.

• • •

Those who *manipulate* see an objection as a stumbling block to change.

Those who *influence* see an objection as an opportunity to continue to problem solve.

• • •

Those who *manipulate* restate benefits to convince others a drawback to their solution isn't necessary.

Those who *influence* restate benefits to help others gain perspective on their solution as a whole.

• • •

Those who *manipulate* struggle with implementation, seeing the mastering of these skills as something they will revisit when it serves them.

Those who *influence* dedicate themselves to implementation, seeing the mastering of these skills as a way to help others in need of change.

• • •

Those who *manipulate* focus exclusively on the strengths of their position.

Those who *influence* focus and analyze both the strengths and weaknesses of their position.

• • •

Those who *manipulate* define victory solely by the change they create.

Those who *influence* define victory by the ethical effort they put forth in their attempts to bring about change.

Acknowledgments

As with any book, there are a lot of people to thank. First, allow me to thank the thousands of salespeople who allowed me to spend the past thirty years of my life teaching, studying, and selling with them. This book is a reflection of the journeys we took together.

My friends at New York Life: You taught me to love selling, and you did this by allowing me to work side by side with some of the greatest salespeople and sales managers I've ever been associated with.

My friends at Xerox: I will always cherish the lessons you taught me, I will always "bleed blue X's" and take pride in being a "Xeroid."

My friend Silvi Brugge: As a reader and editor you had a front-row seat as you helped this book evolve.

My copyeditor Rachel Hockett. Your superb editing skills are obvious, but it's your determination to get it right that makes me grateful to have been teamed up with you.

My children, Danny, Jessie, and Sandy: You not only continue to be a key source of inspiration for everything I do, you make me proud as each of you make your way into this world.

My editor Neal Maillet: You are the only person on the face of this earth whom I implicitly trust to handle my words. Your instinct is uncanny, your scalpel is swift, and your friendship is cherished.

And finally, my wife Ronni: Behind every idea is someone who says, "Yes, you can." Your unwavering belief in me is more important than you could ever know.

Index

Acknowledge stage in decision
cycle, 22–27
commitment to change in,
88–89
decision point in, 24, 25–27
fear of change in, 24–25, 26
number of people in, 37
Acknowledge step in objections
to change, 135–136
and confirming step, 141–145
Active listening, 50–52, 56
behaviors avoided in, 51–52
Aging parents, 11–12
Aim of questions, 52–54, 56, 86
Analytical personality type,
adjustments needed for,
156–157
"And?," as developing probe, 67
Apology avoided in confirming
objections to change,
143–144
Asking questions. *See* Questions
asked

Belief, 6–15
importance of, 7
in sales product, 8–10
Buyer's remorse or reconsider
stage, 34–36, 103
Buying cycle, 18

Cars
decision point in purchase of,
25–26
rental of, 76–78
Change
belief in, 6–15
commitment to, 85–108
confirming benefits of, 98–99
consequences as motivation
for, 80–82
decision cycle in, 17–37
fear of, 7–8, 15, 59
in acknowledge stage,
24–25, 26
objections to change in,
128–129

implementation of process,
149–164
initial conversation on, 109–
125
objections to, 127–147
reassurance on, 104–106
urgency of, 56, 57–83
Cigarette smoking
consequences of, 80–81
decision to quit, 80–81, 86
Clarification of objections to
change, 132–135, 143
Clarification of problem
developing probes in, 65–69,
75, 79, 86
identifying probes in, 60–65,
75, 79
impact probes in, 70–71, 75,
79, 86
Closed questions, 45–46
Commitment to change, 85–108
confirming benefits of, 98–99
discussing logistics of, 102–103
earning the right to ask for,
85, 93–95
methods of asking for, 100–102
myths concerning, 91–97
necessity of asking for, 95–96
reassurance on, 104–106
summary commitment in,
97–108
transition to, 107–108
Communication
facial expressions in, 107
in initial conversation on
change, 109–125
listening in. See Listening
questions asked in. See
Questions asked

tone of, 107
Xerox survey on preferences
in, 42
"you said" response in, 90–91
Confirming benefits of change,
98–99
Confirming objections to change,
141–145
avoiding apology in, 143–144
Confrontational approach
avoided in objections to
change, 132–133
Consequences of actions, 2–3
as motivation, 80–82
Cost, objections to change based
on, 145–147
Criteria stage in decision cycle,
28–31

Decision cycle, 17–37, 86
acknowledge stage in, 22–27,
88–89
affecting implementation of
change process, 151,
152
commitment to change in,
88–89
creating urgency in, 56, 57–83
criteria stage in, 28–31
initial conversation on change
in, 120
investigate stage in, 31–32, 37
reconsider stage in, 34–36, 103
satisfied stage in, 20–22, 37
select stage in, 33–34
Decision-making, strategic, in
implementation of change
process, 150–158
Decision point, 24, 25–27

Developing probes, 65–69, 75, 79, 86
  "And?" as, 67
Disney, Walt, 15
Doctors, influence of, 12–14
Dominant personality type, adjustments needed for, 156
Domonkos, Larry, 69
Drawback objection, 138–140

Einstein, Albert, 44
Empathy, 72, 80
  in objections to change, 137
Enterprise rental cars, 76–78
Ethical issues, 6, 10

Facial expressions, 107
Fear of change, 7–8, 15, 59
  in acknowledge stage, 24–25, 26
  objections to change in, 128–129
"Feel, felt, found" technique
  in objections to change, 137–138
Financial hobby case, 59
  developing probes in, 66
  identifying probes in, 60–61, 63
  impact probes in, 79
  "what if" questions in, 63
Fix, don't fix line, 27
Franklin, Ben, 75

Greed, 112
  and desire for success, 112–113

Home purchase, decision cycle in, 21–24, 28–29, 30–36
Homework hassle case, 97
  asking for commitment in, 101
  confirming benefits in, 99
  discussing logistics in, 103
  reassurance in, 106
Hook step in initiation of change, 111–114, 119
  "what's in it for me" question and answer in, 112
Hostage negotiation, 104–105

Identifying probes, 60–65, 75, 79
  "what if" questions as, 63–64
Impact probes, 70–71, 75, 79, 86
  words used in, 70
Implementation of change process, 149–164
  adjustments to opening conversation in, 155
  anticipation of objections in, 154–155
  anticipation of strengths and weaknesses in, 153–154
  decision cycle stage affecting, 151, 152
  flexibility in tactics used, 152–153
  personality types affecting, 155–160
  strategic decision-making in, 150–158
  worksheet on, 169–170
Influence
  definition of, 1, 85
  empathy in, 72, 80
  flexibility in implementation of process, 149–164

identifying, developing, and
impact probes in, 60–71
initial conversation in, 109–125
intent of, 87
manipulation compared to.
See Manipulation and
influence compared
objections to, 127–147
pitch compared to, 5
trust required for, 39–56
Initial conversation on change,
109–125
anticipation of adjustments
needed in, 155
asking for help in, 121–122
buzzwords avoided in, 124–125
hook in, 111–114, 119
opening in, 109–111, 118–119,
121–123
process in, 114–115, 120
time duration of, 116–118, 120
on value, 122–123
word choices in, 121–125
written preparation for, 118, 155
Insurance sales
belief in, 8–10
decision cycle in, 29
waiting for phone calls in,
29, 63
Intent of influence, 87
Introduction in opening
conversation, 110–111, 119
Investigate stage in decision
cycle, 31–32
number of people in, 37

Lifestyle
of aging parents, 11–12
healthy changes in, 2–3, 12–14

Line in sand or decision point,
24, 25–27
Listening, 41–56, 59
active, 50–52, 56
behaviors avoided in, 51–52
"you said" response in, 90–91
Logistics in commitment to
change, discussions on,
102–103
Lombardi, Vince, 161–162, 163

Management mess case,
objections to change in,
131
acknowledgment of, 135–136
clarification of, 134
confirmation of, 141
drawback, 139–140
"feel, felt, found" technique in,
137–138
Manipulation and influence
compared, 6, 8, 171–174
belief in, 10, 171
commitment to change in, 86,
173
decision process in, 17
empathy in, 80, 172
impact probes on problems in,
70, 172
implementation of change in,
149, 154
initiation of change in, 109,
123–124, 173
intent in, 87
listening in, 59, 172
objections to change in, 127,
140, 173
push in, 62, 172
right question in, 57, 172

trust in, 39, 171
victory and success in, 163, 174
Mays, Billy, 5
Michener, James, 162
Misunderstandings in objections
to change, 136
Motivation for change
consequences of actions in,
80–82
value in, 82

Needs
lack of, objection to change
in, 129–130
and problems, 29, 30–31
"No hurry" objection to change,
130–131
"No need" objection to change,
129–130

Objections to change, 127–147
acknowledgment of, 135–136
anticipation of, 154–155
clarification of, 132–135, 143
confirmation of, 141–145
cost as factor in, 145–147
drawback in, 138–140
in fear of change, 128–129
"feel, felt, found" technique in,
137–138
misunderstandings in, 136
in no hurry, 130–131
in no need, 129–130
response to, 136
Opening conversation for
initiation of change, 106–
111, 118–119
anticipation of adjustments
needed in, 155

asking for help in, 121
introduction to, 110–111, 119
value in, 122–123
written preparation for, 118,
155
Open questions, 45, 46, 49–50,
56
active listening to responses,
50–52
best example of, 49–50
declaration on use of, 46
as identifying probes, 61–62

"Pain" questions, 71–72
Parents, aging, 11–12
Personality types, 155–160
Pitch, 4–6
compared to influence, 5
definition of, 4
Problems
alternative words for, 62
avoiding questions on, 54–55,
56
belief in solutions, 6–15
decision cycle in, 17–37
developing probes on, 65–69,
75, 79, 86
empathy in, 72, 80
identifying probes on, 60–65,
75, 79
impact probes on, 70–71, 75,
79, 86
listening to, 59
and needs, 29, 30–31
urgency of, 56, 57
"what if" questions on, 63–64,
77–78
Procrastination, 59
in acknowledge stage, 24

Push, 3–4, 6
  identifying probes in, 62
  in influence and manipulation
    compared, 62, 172

Questions asked
  active listening to responses
    in, 50–52, 56
  aim of, 52–54, 56, 86
  "and?," 67
  avoiding problems in, 54–55, 56
  closed questions in, 45–46
  on commitment to change, 85,
    87–89, 93–96, 100–102
  developing probes in, 65–69,
    75, 79, 86
  empathy in, 72
  establishing trust in, 41–56
  identifying probes in, 60–65,
    75, 79
  impact probes in, 70–71, 75,
    79, 86
  open questions in. See Open
    questions
  "pain" questions in, 71–72
  sense of urgency created in, 58
  by therapist, 73–75
  "what if," 63–64, 77–78
  "what's in it for me?," 112

Real estate, decision cycle in pur-
    chase of, 21–24, 28–29, 30–36
Reassurance on commitment to
    change, 104–106
Reconsider stage in decision
    cycle, 34–36, 103
Relationship rut case, initial
    conversation on change
    in, 110

hook step in, 113–114
time duration of, 116–117
Resistance to change, 127–147. See
    also Objections to change
Riley, James Whitcomb, 1
Role-playing, 89–90, 153
Roosevelt, Franklin Delano, 51

Sales process
  belief in product affecting, 8–10
  commitment to change in, 93–95
  decision cycle in, 29
  pitch in, 4–6
  as repeatable and predictable,
    18
  trust in, 48
  waiting for phone calls in,
    29, 63
Sanders, Henry "Red," 162
Satisfied stage in decision cycle,
    20–22
  number of people in, 20–21, 37
Select stage in decision cycle,
    33–34
Smith, Dean, 163
Smoking
  consequences of, 80–81
  decision to quit, 80–81, 86
Social personality type,
    adjustments needed for,
    157
Sports in America (Michener), 162
Strategic decision-making in
    implementation of change
    process, 150–158
Success
  and effort, 161–163
  and greed, 112–113
  and winning, 161–163

Summary commitment, 97–108
    asking for commitment in,
        100–102
    confirming benefits in, 98–99
    discussing logistics in, 102–
        103
    reassurance in, 104–106

TCO (total cost of ownership),
    145–147
Therapists, questions asked by,
    73–75
Time duration of initial
    conversation on change,
    116–118, 120
Tone of conversations, 107
Toothbrush example on total cost
    of ownership, 145–146
Total cost of ownership (TCO),
    145–147
Toyota, 53–54
Trust, 39–56
    asking questions and listening
        in creation of, 41–56
    as critical step, 153

Urgency
    creation of, 56, 57–83, 86
    lack of
        in acknowledge stage, 24
        objection to change in,
            130–131
        in providing solutions, 65

Valenti, John, 12–13
Value
    initial conversation on change
        on, 122–123
    as motivation, 82

"What if" questions, 63–64, 77–78
"What's in it for me" question and
    answer in hook step, 112
Whining (acknowledge) stage in
    decision cycle, 22–27
WIFM (what's in it for me), 112
Wilde, Oscar, 143
Winning, and success, 161–163
Word choices
    apology avoided in, 143–144
    buzzwords avoided in, 124–
        125
    in closed questions, 45
    in developing probes, 67
    in impact probes, 70
    in initial conversation on
        change, 121–125
    in open questions, 45, 50
    as substitute for word
        "problem," 62
    in "what if" questions, 63–64,
        77–78
    in "you said" response, 90–91
Written preparation for initial conver-
    sation on change, 118, 155

Xerox
    earning right to ask for
        commitment to change
        in, 93–95
    persuasion method of, 3
    study on asking for
        commitment, 92
    survey on communication
        preferences, 42
    training on sales process in,
        18, 89–90

"You said" response, 90–91

About the Author

Merrill Worthington

A sought-after speaker and best-selling author, Rob Jolles teaches, entertains, and inspires audiences worldwide.

Rob draws on more than thirty years of experience to teach people *how to change minds.* His programs on influence and persuasion are in global demand, reaching organizations in North America, Europe, Africa, and the Far East. And in showing clients not just "how to" but also "why to," he stirs individuals and companies to create real, lasting change.

Today, Rob's keynotes and workshops attract many diverse audiences, from Global 100 companies to growing entrepreneurial enterprises, from parents to professional negotiators. His best-selling books, including *Customer Centered Selling* and *How to Run Seminars & Workshops,* have been translated into more than a dozen languages.

He lives in Great Falls, Virginia.